SECRETS

To Love Life and Be

HAPPY

Powerful Advice with Fun and Insightful Journal Exercises

By Alex A. Lluch
AUTHOR OF OVER 3 MILLION BOOKS SOLD

WS Publishing
www.WSPublishing
San Diego, Californi

D0855500

Secrets to Love Life and Be Happy

By Alex A. Lluch

Published by WS Publishing Group
San Diego, California 92119
Copyright © 2009 by WS Publishing Group

Designed by WS Publishing Group:
David Defenbaugh

Image Credit: © iStockphoto/Diverstudio

For Inquiries:
Log on to www.WSPublishingGroup.com
E-mail info@WSPublishingGroup.com

ISBN: 978-1-934386-52-1

Printed in China

INTRODUCTION

Everyone deserves to be happy and love life, although not all of us know how to reach that state of mind. You may be one of the millions of people who struggle daily with loneliness, sadness, depression, and anxiety. Luckily, being truly happy is often only a matter of adjusting your attitude and perspective and practicing a few simple principles. This book will give you those secrets to enjoying life and being happy. You will find 100 secrets you can implement daily, as well as 100 fun and insightful journaling exercises that can help you make the very most of the wisdom in this book.

By reading this book, you will learn how to make simple but powerful changes in your daily life that will allow you to enjoy life to the fullest. You will learn how to change your perspective to better appreciate all the joy in the world around you. You will learn how to cherish and support your family and friends. You will learn effective ways to reduce stress and anxiety. Finally, you will learn how to love and honor the most important relationship in your life: the one you have with yourself.

Actress Mae West once said, "You only live once, but if you do it right, once is enough." She was absolutely correct in that life is an ongoing process of changing, discovering, making mistakes, and moving forward. Delve into the secrets and exercises in this book; carry it with you in your purse or car and refer to it when you need a pick-me-up or reminder for how to enjoy life. By exploring the secrets in this book, you will be well on your way to experiencing all the happiness, harmony, love, and joy that life has waiting for you.

Smile — even when you don't feel like it.

Even if you don't feel like it, smile. It can make you feel and look better, instantly, because smiling releases endorphins, natural pain killers produced by the brain.

In addition, put positive thinking behind your smile; a recent study by the Wake Forest University Baptist Medical Center found that thinking positively actually helps people overcome pain! In fact, Dr. Tetsuo Koyama, the lead author of the study, said, "Positive expectations produced about a 28 percent decrease in pain ratings — equal to a shot of morphine."

Finally, wearing a smile is infectious. You will find that your friends and coworkers respond more positively to you, and also start grinning themselves. As it has been said: "A smile is an inexpensive way to change your looks."

So smile — it is a simple way to change the way you look and feel from the outside in.

How good are you at putting on a happy face, even when you are feeling down?

_____

_____

_____

_____

Write down the names of 3 people you know who are always smiling. How does seeing those people make you feel?

Person 1:

_____

_____

Person 2:

_____

_____

Person 3:

_____

_____

Now that you have tried smiling, even when you don't feel like it, reflect on how it has positively affected your mood and the ways others respond to you. Have you found it easy or difficult to do?

_____

_____

_____

_____

_____

Focus on the things that are great in your life.

An old Swedish proverb states, "Worry often gives a small thing a big shadow." Indeed, we make mountains out of molehills by needlessly obsessing over things that are imperfect in our lives. Resist the urge to fixate on what you want to change about yourself or your circumstances.

Staying present in your own life is the best way to be happy in it. When you feel jealous of someone else's life or circumstances, focus, instead, on taking stock of what you do have and be thankful for it.

Concentrate on the things that are great in your life, and channel your energy into those areas. Maybe you are really excelling in your guitar lessons or are spending time with a wonderful new friend. Affirming the good aspects of life allows them to flourish and gives you energy to improve other areas that may need more attention.

How often do you compare yourself to others and feel jealous? Very often? Occasionally? Never?

Make a list of the things you have to be thankful for:

2 people in my life I am grateful for:

2 things I like about my job:

2 things I like about my appearance:

2 skills or talents I have:

How has concentrating on being thankful helped you keep feelings of jealousy in check?

Don't sweat the small stuff.

The line at the bank may be 20 people long. Your spouse may forget to pick up your clothes from the dry cleaner. A friend may flake on lunch plans at the last moment. Traffic might be a nightmare. It is tempting to get upset, but, more often than not, these things are small things that are easy to let go. Not sweating the small stuff means evaluating how important a grievance is to you and assessing how willing you are to get angry or engage in an argument over it.

The next time a situation arises, here are some questions you should ask yourself to avoid a fight:

- "Is this issue really worth getting angry over?"
- "Will I still care about this a month from now?"
- "Is anything positive going to come of this argument?"

If you answer no to any of these questions, you can probably just say, "No problem," instead of getting angry.

Picking your battles wisely will keep you from feeling stressed out over petty things. Instead, read a magazine in line at the bank. Find a good song on the radio during a traffic jam. And, always give the people in your life much-needed room to be human; hopefully, they'll do the same for you.

How good are you at letting small things go? Do you find yourself in petty arguments often?

Think of 3 past instances where you could have avoided an argument with a friend, coworker, or family member by letting a minor thing slide.

Instance 1:

Instance 2:

Instance 3:

Reflect on how you've been practicing not sweating the small stuff. What types of things have been easy to let go? What situations have been a challenge?

Get outside your comfort zone.

Often, we struggle with boredom and unhappiness because we have fallen into a rut. After a while, people are less interested in working at their relationships and their own well-being. However, you should never become complacent with your life. To truly enjoy life, you must get outside your comfort zone.

A great concept to live by is to try something that scares you every day, be it speaking in front of a crowd, rock climbing, or asking the girl at the coffee shop for her phone number.

Trying new things outside your comfort zone shows your sense of confidence and adventure and keeps life from ever feeling dull and routine. Your friends may even find you to be an inspiration!

How comfortable are you with trying something outside your comfort zone? How often do you do something new? Once a week? Once a month? Almost never?

Make a list of 10 things you can do to get outside your comfort zone.

1.
2.
3
4.
5.
6.
7.
8.
9.
10.

What was the last thing outside your comfort zone you tried? Reflect on the experience: How did you feel? What did the experience offer you?

SECRET 5

Be open to spontaneous moments.

Sociologist Helen Merrell Lynd said that spontaneity should be "an expression of our deepest desires and values." Enjoying life requires creativity and a willingness to discover the opportunities for adventure that are all around us. Boredom can be much like a car that runs on fumes — you neglect to add gas to the car and it sputters to a stop.

Being spontaneous takes you out of your comfort zone and helps you discover new interests. It is amazing how much trying a new recipe, hobby, sport, restaurant, or movie genre can change your mood.

Spontaneity is simply expressing a joy for life, so be open to all opportunities that arise. Remind yourself that your regular life and all its demands will be there when you get back. If you see a festival, fair, or parade is happening in your neighborhood, drop everything and just go. Should you drive by a beautiful beach, stop and stick your feet in the sand. Strive to be the kind of person who is always willing to go on a small adventure at the spur of the moment.

How spontaneous are you? What has kept you from being spontaneous in the past?

You can take advantage of spontaneous opportunities by packing a bag that you keep in your car or at work so you will be ready for a day at the beach or an impromptu hike at a moment's notice. List the kinds of things you would include. Then go pack your bag!

Reflect on your newfound spontaneity: How has being spontaneous helped you better enjoy life?

SECRET 6

Practice forgiveness to lighten your load.

Holding on to resentment is extremely unhealthy and can cause chronic health and emotional problems. Lighten your load by contacting someone you need to forgive and letting the person know that he or she has been forgiven. It is best to meet in person and speak face-to-face. If this is not possible, call this person on the phone or send a handwritten letter. Acknowledge that your feelings have been hurt, but that you are ready and willing to forgive. If an apology is given, allow the freedom that comes from forgiveness to set in. Realize that it won't happen overnight. Forgiveness can be a slow process for many of us, but you will feel a weight lifted from your shoulders after you have truly forgiven.

Forgiving does not mean that you must forget the event or that you are condoning bad behavior. It simply means you set yourself free from negativity, bitterness, and anger. You will be able to move forward to a better place in your life. As Ph.D. Robert Karen writes, "True forgiveness isn't easy, but it transforms us significantly." Feeling free through forgiveness is one of the many keys to being a more joyful person.

Has forgiveness been a challenge for you in the past? Why or why not? What are some obstacles to forgiveness for you?

Think of someone you need to forgive. How can you approach forgiving this person? What will you say or do to ease the process of forgiveness?

Describe your recent attempt at forgiveness. How did it go? How did you feel after you truly forgave the person?

Make a heartfelt apology to someone you have wronged.

A heartfelt apology can go a long way in healing wounds. Apologizing when appropriate will also free you from guilt and shame, which are major obstacles to happiness.

Most friendships and relationships become stronger after an argument that ends with a heartfelt apology. Strong relationships are built on a foundation of trust, which comes from knowing a person can take responsibility for themselves and also graciously accept flaws in others. Don't be afraid to take the initiative to apologize to anyone you may have hurt or wronged.

There are several things to remember when crafting your apologies. First, when someone tells you that you have hurt his or her feelings, listen intently. Fight the urge to become defensive. Don't get bogged down in the details of the event; focus on what you did or said that was hurtful. Finally, take responsibility, be humble, and apologize sincerely.

Through this process, you will obtain personal growth, strength of character, and the respect of others.

Do you always apologize when necessary? Do you find it easy or difficult to apologize?

Think of someone whom you owe an apology. What would you like say to him or her?

Describe the apology you gave and how it made you feel. Was it difficult, scary, easy, or a relief?

Incorporate positive affirmations into your daily routine.

Use positive affirmations to reprogram negative thoughts. For instance, instead of telling yourself, "I will never be happy," think, "I am content at this moment." Over time, these affirmations will add up to a powerful collection of positive thoughts and mindsets. Not only will affirming the positive give you higher-quality days, but more of them. A recent study by researchers at the Mayo Clinic found that people who think positively live 19 percent longer than those who do not.

Tell yourself something from this list several times a day. Focus on the words and how it feels to make positive statements about yourself. When you feel the urge to say, "This is stupid," force yourself to replace that thought with one of the affirmations below.

- I am smart
- I am capable
- I am doing my best
- I am a good person
- I am fun
- I am proud of myself
- I forgive myself
- I will succeed

- I am happy
- I am loving
- I am grateful
- I accept my flaws
- I have many strengths
- I am entitled to happiness
- I like my body
- I deserve respect from others

What are your most common negative thoughts?

Write down a list of positive affirmations you can use to replace your common negative thoughts.

How has using positive affirmations changed your daily outlook? Reflect on positive changes in your attitude.

SECRET 9

Use visualization techniques to improve your outlook.

Rhonda Byrne's book *The Secret* became a best-seller overnight. But the book's premise is no secret at all. According to *The Secret*, the key to happiness and success is to picture yourself as a happy and successful person. Use visualization techniques to achieve this. Visualization can help you refocus and see your goals clearly. Visualization helps you believe in yourself and make your goals realistic and attainable.

Build a positive outlook on your future by practicing the following visualization exercises:

- Find a magazine and tear out a picture of an amazing place you would like to visit or have a second home. Visualizing yourself there will motivate you to take the necessary steps to make it a reality — be it sticking to a budget, saving wisely, or begin planning a vacation.

- Visualize yourself at your ideal weight. See yourself being active — exercising, dancing, or walking, for instance. See yourself at the beach wearing a new swimsuit. Feel the confidence you have. Create a new reality!

What goals would you like to make a reality? Examples might be getting a promotion at work, losing 20 pounds, or saving for a down payment on a house.

_____

_____

_____

_____

_____

What visualization techniques can you use to change your outlook and reach your goals?

_____

_____

_____

_____

_____

_____

_____

How have visualization techniques been a success? How have they improved your outlook on life?

_____

_____

_____

_____

_____

_____

Look in the mirror and find several things you love.

According to Planet Project, a global Internet polling company that polled 380,000 people in more than 225 countries, just 35 percent of all people enjoy the view when they look in the mirror. That means when 65 percent of the world's population looks in the mirror, they are disappointed!

Improve your outlook by enjoying what you see. Look in the mirror each morning and find several things about yourself that you love. Say, "I have nice eyes," "I like the way my hair looks today," or "My teeth are very white." After a while, you will learn to love the whole image.

Remember, no one will be able to appreciate and enjoy your unique beauty if you don't love it yourself. On the contrary, when you feel attractive and confident, people will see you in the same light.

How do you feel when you look in the mirror? Are you pleased, satisfied, or unhappy with your appearance?

Name several things you can appreciate about your unique look and features.

Describe one thing about your appearance you have come to appreciate.

Start a weekly Gratitude Journal.

The way we view things is a by-product of our daily experiences. We all have positive experiences every day but many of us concentrate on the negative ones. However, daily gratitude will help you live life to the fullest and appreciate even the smallest moments of joy.

Start keeping a Gratitude Journal: Each week, make a list of your positive experiences and happy moments. No enjoyment is too small to write down. Examples might be if you tried a new flavor of coffee, took a relaxing walk, or found a shortcut that reduces your commute to work by 10 minutes. At the end of the week, notice how many little joys life presented in just a matter of days.

As the saying goes, "Gratitude is the least of virtues; ingratitude the worst of vices." You will find that appreciating the small things you have to be grateful for will pave the way for bigger triumphs.

Have you ever kept a log or journal of your daily experiences? If yes, how did it make you feel?

Write down several recent occurrences or experiences that you can add to your Gratitude Journal.

After a few weeks of keeping your Gratitude Journal, reflect on how it has benefited you and your happiness. Have you discovered that you, in fact, have more to be grateful for than you anticipated?

Celebrate other people's successes to make way for your own windfalls.

Even though you may have a lot to be grateful for in your life, it is not uncommon to feel a twinge of jealousy or even bitterness when others experience success or triumph. Practice being the first to congratulate a friend, even if he or she receives something you wanted for yourself. This is the best way to take power away from ugly feelings of jealousy or insecurity when something good happens to someone else.

For instance, if a friend calls to say she is engaged, instead of asking internally, "Why didn't this happen to me?" say out loud, "I'm so happy for you!" Or, if a coworker announces he got a promotion, offer to help him celebrate by having lunch or a celebratory drink.

As author Melody Beattie has said, "[Gratitude] can turn a meal into a feast, a house into a home, a stranger into a friend." Truly, being a supportive friend paves the way for your own windfalls.

Describe a time when someone announced their success and you felt resentful or jealous. Why do you think you felt that way? How did you react to the news?

Come up with a situation where you can practice rejoicing in another's success. Then, write down what you would say or do to help show your support.

Have you been able to rejoice in other people's good fortune? Check off all the following benefits you have experienced.

❑ Less jealousy
❑ Less resentment
❑ Hopefulness
❑ Motivation

❑ Gratitude
❑ Sharing in other's joy
❑ Happiness
❑ Reduced stress

Express frustration before it boils over.

Frustration and hurt, if not released, quickly lead to high levels of stress and unhappiness. It is a good idea to deal with small annoyances as they come up rather than waiting until you explode with rage. Think of a kettle filled with hot water. If you don't release some of the steam, the kettle will start to hiss and boil over. Talking about frustration prevents anger from boiling over into a larger problem.

It is very important to address behaviors, not personality traits. For instance, if you criticize your spouse by saying, "I am the only one who empties the dishwasher around here," he or she will get angry or withdraw. On the contrary, your spouse will be more likely to respond positively if you address the behavior and politely say, "I would really appreciate if we could both pitch in to help with the dishes."

In most cases, you will get cooperation if you express frustration early on and do not personalize the problem.

Do you tend to let annoyances build up and the boil over, or do you address them along the way?

Rework the following phrases so you address the behavior and do not attack the person:

"You're so lazy; you always leave dirty dishes in the sink."

"You're late again."

"My feelings obviously aren't important to you."

"You never return my calls."

Reflect on a recent instance when you were successful in addressing a person's behavior and asking politely for it to change. Describe what you said and how the person reacted.

SECRET 14

Adopt a "who cares" attitude.

Journalist Sydney J. Harris once asked, "If a small thing has the power to make you angry, does that not indicate something about your size?" Indeed, only small, petty people are ruffled by small, petty events. Show those around you the depth of your character by refusing to become undone by minor obstacles.

For example, if you are stuck standing in a long line at the bank, make conversation with the person ahead of you. If you accidentally make a wrong turn, enjoy a good song on the radio to pass the extra time. If your partner burns dinner, laugh it off and order takeout.

Being carefree and untroubled is emblematic of someone who is young at heart and delights in life. People are inspired by those who appear joyous, carefree, and happy.

How skilled are you at adopting a "who cares" attitude? Do you let small things roll off your back, or do you get upset easily?

Think of 3 situations where you might be tempted to lose your cool, but could try reacting with a "who cares" attitude instead.

Situation 1:

Situation 2:

Situation 3:

How has using a "who cares" attitude made your life easier and happier?

Give back to your community.

Anne Frank wrote in her famous diary, "How wonderful it is that nobody need wait a single moment before starting to improve the world." Truly, enjoying life and being happy means contributing positively to your community. The time you give to others is often as valuable to them as money.

Giving your time to a worthy cause also helps put your own problems in perspective, gives you a sense of belonging within a community, and enhances your sense of self-worth. Studies show that people who devote at least 1 to 2 hours per week to a worthy cause feel an immediate boost in their self-confidence, happiness, and sense of purpose.

Sign up for one of the countless opportunities to volunteer in your community. Websites that can help you find a good fit for you include www.volunteermatch.org, www.voa.org, and www. usafreedomcorps.gov.

Serving your community will remind you that you have a purpose larger than yourself, and help you feel grateful for everything you have.

How have you given back to your community in the past? What types of philanthropic work do you enjoy?

Here are some great ways to serve your community. Check off the opportunities that appeal to you!

- ❑ Volunteer at a homeless shelter
- ❑ Write letters to soldiers
- ❑ Pick up trash around your neighborhood
- ❑ Help out at an animal shelter
- ❑ Build houses in a low-income area
- ❑ Adopt a less-fortunate family during the holidays
- ❑ Donate clothing, blankets, or toys to a shelter
- ❑ Serve meals at a soup kitchen

How did your volunteering experiences make you feel about yourself and your community? How do you plan to continue giving back in the future?

SECRET
16

Practice Feng Shui in your home.

According to the ancient Chinese practice of Feng Shui, the choices you make when decorating affect your happiness and quality of life. Implement Feng Shui by removing the clutter in your home, which blocks the flow of positive energy, or chi.

Observe these rules of Feng Shui when cleaning and rearranging your home:

- Avoid dark colors and heavy curtains that may weigh you down and anchor your mood
- Use mirrors to make rooms look larger, but never place one directly across from your bed
- Place flowering plants in groups of 3 near the entrance to your home
- Remove any dead, dried flowers
- Don't have a television in your bedroom
- Don't leave shoes by the front door
- Place an indoor water fountain in your home
- Clear kitchen countertops. Store appliances, like the toaster, when they are not in use

By practicing the principles of Feng Shui, your home will become a breezeway for positive energy.

What are some problems areas or obstacles to healthy energy flow in your home?

How can you incorporate the principles of Feng Shui to make your home more open for the flow of positive energy?

Reflect on your newly Feng Shui'd home. How do you feel now that your home is free from clutter?

SECRET 17

Commit a Random Act of Kindness.

The concept of Random Acts of Kindness gained popularity in the 1990s, even sparking a foundation by the same name. The idea is that with either planned or spontaneous acts of kindness, either toward friends or strangers, people can effect positive change in their communities and well as inspire others to pass kindness on.

Random Acts of Kindness need not be spontaneous, though you should leave yourself open to the possibility of doing something kind for others at any moment. Examples include:

- Compliment a stranger.
- Help someone with a flat tire.
- Make dinner for a neighbor with a new baby.
- Do a favor for a friend, such as offering to help him or her move.

Committing a Random Act of Kindness will make you feel wonderful and will open you up to the possibility for more good in your life.

What Random Acts of Kindness have you performed in the past? How did you feel afterwards?

Come up with 10 random acts you can do daily or weekly.

1.
2.
3.
4.
5.
6.
7.
8.
9.
10.

Reflect on the random acts you committed.

Organize a food drive.

Everyone should be able to eat three meals a day but, unfortunately, many people go without. The National Coalition for the Homeless estimates there are as many as 3.5 million homeless in the U.S., 39 percent of whom are children. Surveys by the Coalition and partner organizations found that 40 percent of homeless go at least one day a month with nothing to eat. You can help those less fortunate than you by organizing a food drive.

Start by contacting a local shelter and asking what items they need most. Then, organize a group of volunteers and coordinate a drop-off site. This can be as simple as setting out a box in your store or office and collecting canned and dry goods. Make sure you publicize your food drive to friends and family and have them spread the word around the community.

Organizing a food drive is an excellent way to give back to your community and will also help you feel a real sense of accomplishment and gratitude.

Have you participated in a food drive in the past? How much did you invest yourself in it? How did your participation make you feel?

Make a list of what you will need to do to organize a food drive. Think about things like how you will advertise your food drive to the public and your goals for the drive.

How successful was your effort? Did you meet your goals? What personal benefits did you get from the drive?

Get a great night's sleep.

Getting at least 8 hours of sleep every night is important to your overall well-being. Studies consistently show that lack of sleep or sleeping at odd hours heightens the risk for a variety of major illnesses, including cancer, heart disease, and diabetes. Additionally, not getting enough of sleep leads to stress and overeating. In fact, research has shown adults between the ages of 32 and 49 who sleep less than 7 hours a night are significantly more likely to be obese.

So grab that extra sleep when you can! Avoid tossing and turning over what has been left undone by taking care of pressing tasks before you go to bed. If you feel too tired to attend to everything before you sleep, make a list of what needs to be done and resolve to finish everything the next day.

Getting a full night's sleep will give you added energy and allow you to make the most of your days.

How many hours of sleep do you get each night? Do you need to sleep more? What are your obstacles to sleep?

Here is a list of tips and tricks for getting a good night's sleep. Check off the ones you can implement to sleep better:

- ❏ Don't exercise within an hour before bed
- ❏ Avoid caffeine after 5 p.m.
- ❏ Write down a list of things that are on your mind, then trust yourself to deal with them the next day
- ❏ Skip alcohol or have only 1 glass of wine
- ❏ Make your bedroom a sanctuary — meaning no TV, no work, and no bills in the room
- ❏ Read for 15 minutes in bed to help you relax
- ❏ Don't smoke. Nicotine is a stimulant!
- ❏ Avoid having a large meal right before bedtime
- ❏ Stick to a regular sleep schedule. Even on the weekends!

Write about any new habits and how they have helped you get a better night's sleep.

SECRET
20

Limit caffeine and sugar intake.

According to Johns Hopkins University School of Medicine, 80 to 90 percent of North American adults and more than 165 million Americans report using caffeine regularly. In fact, caffeine is the world's most commonly used drug. However, caffeine and sugar can also lead to rapid heart rate, feelings of anxiety and irritability, and increased fatigue after the effects wear off.

When you feel tired and need a lift, avoid reaching for caffeine and sugar. Caffeine will give you a quick jolt of energy that will quickly fade and leave you tired again and craving more caffeine. There are many ways to reenergize without the harmful and negative after-effects of overindulging in caffeine and sugar.

Replace your mid-morning coffee with a vigorous, 10-minute walk. This will increase circulation and energize your body.

Or, replace caffeine and sugar with complex carbohydrates and healthy snacks that help maintain levels of serotonin, a mood-elevating chemical in the brain. Eating healthy foods will boost your mood and maintain your energy without relying on caffeine and sugar.

How much caffeine and sugar do you consume daily? Have you found your intake affects your performance and mood, either positively or negatively?

Find healthy substitutions for caffeine and sugar. Check off options that appeal to you as alternatives:

- Caffeine alternatives
    - ❏ Green tea (lower levels of caffeine and a myriad of health benefits)

- Complex carbs
    - ❏ Fruits
    - ❏ Vegetables
    - ❏ Whole grains

- Light, healthy snacks
    - ❏ Yogurt
    - ❏ Nuts
    - ❏ Protein bar

- Re-up your energy naturally
    - ❏ Take a brisk walk
    - ❏ Stretch for 10 minutes
    - ❏ Take a 15-minute nap

How do you feel since reducing your caffeine and sugar intake?

Learn the art of deep breathing.

Deep breathing is an excellent practice that promotes more oxygen flow to your brain and lymphatic system and releases endorphins, the body's natural pain killers and relaxants.

First, sit with your back straight. Exhale completely through your mouth, making a whoosh sound. Close your mouth and inhale quietly through your nose to a mental count of four. Hold your breath for a count of seven. Exhale completely through your mouth, making a whoosh sound to a count of eight. This is one breath. Now inhale again and repeat the cycle three more times for a total of four breaths.

Deep breathing is a natural tranquilizer for the nervous system. Once you develop this technique by practicing it every day it will be a very useful tool that you can use at any time. Use it whenever anything upsetting happens, before you react. Use it whenever you are aware of internal tension. Use it to help you fall asleep. When you are angry, deep breathing will ease you into a state of physical calm, and your mood will surely follow.

What techniques do you typically use to relax? Have you practiced deep breathing in the past?

You should try and carve out 15 minutes of each day to be quiet with your thoughts and practice deep breathing. When might that be beneficial, such as during the middle of your workday?

How has practicing deep breathing techniques helped you relax and relieve stress?

Meditate to relieve stress.

Meditation quiets the mind, which enables you to concentrate and think clearly for longer periods of time. Research shows that meditation also increases cardiovascular and respiratory health as well as boosts the immune system. One study followed the health of more than 2,000 people over a 5-year period. Researchers found that those who meditated had more than 50 percent fewer doctor visits than did non-meditators of similar age, gender, and profession.

Meditation is a wonderful stress-relieving exercise, because it can be done easily, quickly, inexpensively, and almost anywhere. Meditation instantly calms you by increasing blood flow and slowing the heart rate, and just 5 minutes of it can have powerful healing and restorative effects. According to the National Institutes of Health, "Meditation techniques offer the potential of learning how to live in an increasingly complex and stressful society while helping to preserve health in the process."

So find a quiet spot, sit comfortably, and imagine a peaceful place. Take slow, deep breaths. Clear your mind of all stressors. In no time, meditation may become your favorite way to relax!

Have you ever practiced meditation in the past? How did it affect or benefit you?

Think of a time and a place where you might set aside 5 to 15 minutes for daily meditation.

Write down the benefits you experienced from meditation. Do you feel happier, more peaceful, less stressed?

Exercise daily to give your body a natural high!

Daily exercise has myriad benefits, including relieving stress, boosting your self-esteem, and, of course, combating illness and disease. Additionally, regular physical activity can spark your sex life! When you exercise, your body releases endorphins, which naturally boost your mood and give you more stamina. Plus, a lean, toned body can increase your confidence in the bedroom. So, be sure to incorporate 30 minutes of physical activity into your daily routine.

While most of us know the benefits of exercise, many of us think we are too busy. With so much to gain, you should always make exercise a priority in your schedule. Besides, working out doesn't have to mean joining a gym. You can find activities that you enjoy that don't require a gym, such as hiking, rollerblading, or swimming.

Stop making excuses for skipping exercise and start finding solutions. There are physical activities for everyone, of all fitness levels! And everyone can enjoy the rewards of daily exercise.

How active are you currently? List some physical activities that you enjoy that you can incorporate on a daily or weekly basis.

Identify and eliminate your biggest obstacles to exercise. Write down your top excuses for avoiding exercise, then, jot down a few ways to overcome each excuse. An example:

Excuse: "I don't have enough time."
Resolve: Use half of my lunch break to go for a brisk walk.

Excuse 1:
Resolve 1:

Excuse 2:
Resolve 2:

Excuse 3:
Resolve 3:

Were you able to incorporate new kinds of physical activity into your daily routine? What are your future goals for exercise?

Quit smoking right now.

Quitting smoking is difficult, but the frightening truth is, about half of all smokers who continue will end up dying from a smoking-related illness. Quitting smoking greatly reduces your risk for developing respiratory ailments, heart disease, and smoking-related cancers. And did you know that quitting smoking can boost your sex life? Nicotine tightens blood vessels and restricts blood flow, lessening arousal in women and putting men at risk for impotence. Former smokers consistently testify that they are much happier than when they smoked. By quitting smoking today, you will instantly be healthier and better able to enjoy life.

Below are some tips and tricks you can use to start quitting for life today. Visit www.cdc.gov/tobacco to get additional help.

- Taper off: Start smoking 1 hour later each day and stop 1 hour earlier.
- Throw out all ashtrays in your home.
- Tell your friends, family, and coworkers you are quitting. Have them check up on you and hold you accountable. You will be more inclined to stick to your plan if you share with others.
- Write up a quit contract for yourself.

Like most smokers, you have probably tried to quit many times, unsuccessfully. Write about the last time you tried to quit and the obstacles that prevented your success.

Identifying your smoking triggers can help you quit. For instance, are there certain people or environments that make you crave a cigarette? Or do certain foods or beverages—such as red meat, alcohol, or coffee—trigger a craving? Make a list of your triggers here:

Detail why you want to quit smoking. A reason might be that you want to be healthy for your family, or that you want to run a marathon. These statements will serve as motivators.

Allow friends and family to care for you when you are down.

Dealing with sadness and hardship is something everyone will encounter at some point. Don't try and deal with heartache or loss alone. When you are feeling down and find you have trouble coping, let your friends and family know so they can help you. Mourning alone is difficult and can even prolong depression if you lose touch with the outside world. Although you may be in pain, strive to stay connected with others as you cope.

During the really trying times, rely on friends and family to help you rest, relax, and rejuvenate. Allow your loved ones to care for you in any way they offer. Sit down with a friend who listens quietly. Make the person understand he or she doesn't have to offer advice, just listen. Accept a shoulder to lean on and have a good, cathartic cry. Or, they can do simple things for you, such as bring over dinner or do a load of laundry. Acknowledge the help and accept it gratefully.

As philosopher Kahlil Gibran once wrote, "Sadness is but a wall between two gardens." Good times are sure to resurface with the help of your loved ones.

Acknowledge a time when you could have used the help of others, but were afraid or embarrassed to ask. Reflect on how that time felt.

Come up with a list of simple ways people in your life might help you through a tough time. Return to this list as a reminder that help and love are all around you.

Think of a time when you did allow a friend or loved one to come to your aid. Reflect on what he or she did and how it affected you.

Honor a loved one you have lost.

Losing a loved one is devastating, and grief can be a long and difficult process. However, remembering a loved one does not have to be sad or depressing; you can rejoice in happy memories of friends and family who have passed by honoring them in your daily life.

When you are missing your mother, eat at her favorite restaurant or make a recipe she loved. If a friend has passed away, make a donation to her favorite charity in her name. Or, if your grandfather enjoyed fishing, take a fishing trip and think of him fondly.

When you honor a lost loved one, you allow the person's legacy to continue to bless your life. This practice will help you feel close to him or her, and you will take a wonderful step toward happiness and joy.

What are a few ways in which you already honor or celebrate someone you have lost?

Think of one person whose life you can celebrate by creating a new tradition. What might you do?

Has honoring this person helped you cope with sadness or grief? Do you feel happier as a result?

SECRET 27

Make a date — with yourself.

You must work to nurture the most important relationship you have — the one with yourself. Many of us go out of our way to do nice things for others but neglect our own happiness and well-being. In addition, studies have shown that Americans are some of the most stressed out people in the world. Carving out some time for a solo date can help you better enjoy life.

Block out some time just for you, and honor the commitment. If something comes up, treat the time you have planned with yourself as any other appointment, and keep it. See a movie, enjoy a homemade dinner and a glass of wine, or stay in and take a hot bath.

Nurturing the relationship you have with yourself brings daily joy and is the model for the happy relationships you have with others. When you make time for you, you relieve the stress in your life, thus making you a better coworker, friend, and family member.

Can you think of the last time you took an afternoon or even an hour to pamper or treat yourself?

Describe your perfect date with yourself.

How did you benefit from your solo date? What did you do?

Show appreciation for the important people in your life.

Marcel Proust once wrote, "Let us be grateful to people who make us happy; they are the charming gardeners who make our souls blossom." In truth, most people remember special days such as birthdays and anniversaries of the ones they love. But you should also select other occasions to show special people in your life how much they mean to you. This will greatly enhance and deepen your relationships.

For instance, when shopping, pick up an extra treat for your mother. Plan an unexpected movie night for you and a good friend. Bring home dinner from your wife's favorite restaurant to show her how much you care.

What you do to express your appreciation is not as important as the thought behind it. Unexpected, thoughtful acts will inject new energy into your relationships and happiness in your life.

Do you feel you do enough to show appreciation for the special people in your life?

Make a list of the people you would like to do something nice and unexpected for. Then write how you will show your appreciation for them.

Reflect on how the people close to you reacted to you showing your appreciation.

Thank your parents for everything they have done for you.

Raising children is never easy — a fact that we may not fully understand until we have our own families. Children definitely do not come with an instruction manual. Finances may be strained, or both parents may not be present. However, despite the many challenges your parents probably faced, odds are, they did the best job they could raising you. There is much to thank them for — everything from ballet lessons to financial help to offering their unconditional love and support.

No matter who you are, there are things you can admire and respect about your parents, so call them and thank them for being there for you over the years. Expressing your gratitude is both a way to show your appreciation and acknowledge what a tough job being a parent is. You will find it quite uplifting to thank them for all they have done.

What are some obstacles and challenges you imagine your parents faced in raising you?

Create a list of things you would like to thank your parents for. Now tell them how you feel!

Describe your parents' reaction to you thanking them.

Say no if you're in over your head.

Having too many obligations is sure to stress anyone out! Therefore, it is important to say no and set boundaries at times. Saying no will not only reduce stress but keep you healthy. According to the Centers for Disease Control, the leading 6 causes of death in the U.S. — heart disease, cancer, lung ailments, accidents, cirrhosis of the liver, and suicide — are all brought on at least in part by stress.

Though it is nice to be invited to things, it is not necessary to accept every invitation. Find a polite way to decline. Similarly, if a friend asks a favor of you, and you simply don't have the time, apologize, but decline.

Know what your limits are and stick to them. Setting boundaries is essential in achieving healthy and peaceful relationships. As poet Robert Frost wrote, "Good fences make good neighbors." For example, let people know your house is a "no-call zone" during dinnertime, or respectfully tell people your schedule is full for the week.

Feel empowered to say no when it is appropriate and in your best interest. Love yourself enough to set limits on what can be demanded of you.

How skilled are you at saying no? Do you accept invitations or agree to help, even when it is a strain on your time and energy?

Think of a few instances when you would like to say no. Write down what you might say to respectfully decline an offer.

How did it feel to say no? Did you feel more relaxed? Did you find more time for yourself or your loved ones?

Pick a room in your house and organize it.

Being organized reduces the stress that comes from not knowing where to find something in a pinch. Additionally, clutter takes up physical space and negatively affects your mental health and happiness. So, choose your bedroom, the garage, the kitchen, or any other room in your house and organize it to give you a sense of order and satisfaction.

After you have removed some of the clutter in the room, find a place for everything. Organize desk drawers. Hang coats on hooks. Fold and put away laundry. Mount tools on a wall-rack in the garage.

Also, you will most likely discover you have more stuff than you have room for, so create boxes of clothes, toys, furniture, and appliances and donate them to a secondhand or thrift store.

Once your giveaways have a new home and the room is arranged in an organized fashion, you will feel much more relaxed and happy. This sense of accomplishment may inspire you to tackle every room in the house!

On a scale of 1 to 10, rate how organized the various rooms in your home are currently:

Bedrooms:

Bathrooms:

Living room:

Kitchen:

Closets:

Garage:

Other:

Choose one room to start with. Detail your plan to organize this space.

Describe the changes you made to this room. How do you feel now that this room is neat and organized?

SECRET 32

Create a list of things you want to do in your lifetime.

One way to plan to enjoy life to the fullest is to create a list of things you want to do in your lifetime. Some will be simple, such as "try a new cuisine" or "camp out under the stars." Others may call for some planning, such as "plant a garden," "get to know my neighbors," or "build a wine collection." Still other things on your list will require lots of foresight and preparation, such as "hike through a rainforest," "visit the Great Wall of China," or "learn to scuba dive."

Don't limit yourself, as you have your entire life to complete everything on your list. The wonderful part of this exercise is you get to dream — either alone, with friends, or with your spouse — and plan for future adventures.

As Dr. Seuss once playfully wrote, "If you never did you should. These things are fun and fun is good!" So make your list, and get excited about the possibilities ahead of you.

Make a list of 20 things you would like to do in your lifetime.

1.

2.

3.

4.

5.

6.

7.

8.

9.

10.

11.

12.

13.

14.

15.

16.

17.

18.

19.

20.

What are some first steps you can take to complete this list?

Laugh out loud often.

Studies show that laughter reduces stress, lowers blood pressure, elevates mood, and boosts the immune system. Laughter also improves brain functioning, increases oxygen in the blood, fosters connection with others, and makes you feel good all over.

In addition, the American College of Cardiology has found that the short-term positive effects of laughing last for up to 45 minutes. Researchers recommend 15 minutes of laughter a day, as well as regular exercise, to promote cardiovascular health.

Children in nursery school laugh approximately 300 times a day, while adults laugh only about 17 times per day. Why should children reap all the benefits? See a funny movie, read a daily joke, or just share a laugh with friends. Incorporate a good chuckle into your day to reduce stress and promote relaxation and happiness.

Do you feel that you laugh often enough? Why or why not?

Create a list of things that make you laugh that you can seek out in your daily life. Then, go do them!

How have you actively sought out laughter in your life? Reflect on any health benefits you have experienced.

Expand your social circle!

To increase happiness and extend your life, incorporate new and interesting people into your social circle. A recent study published in the *Journal of Epidemiology and Community Health* found that having a network of good friends can extend a person's lifespan. Another study linked positive, nurturing friendships with healthier exercise, diet, and sleeping habits.

Gravitate toward friends with similar values, goals, and interests and who share your positive attitude about life. Meet new people while doing the things you love, be that playing a sport, shopping, or attending a book club.

All your friends should give you a sense of support and belonging. Invigorating friendships will benefit your health, attitude, and emotional well-being, so expand your social circle to better enjoy life.

Are you happy with your current circle of friends? Or, are you looking to meet new friends? If you are dissatisfied with your social circle, describe why.

Brainstorm places you might go or activities you might do that will allow you to meet new friends.

Describe one new friend you have made recently. Where did you meet? Why are you excited about this new friendship?

Educate yourself about your fears.

Fear is much more than just a mental state. Fear can cause extreme stress on the body and mind, including increased heart rate, sweating, loss of vision, and shortness of breath, as well as poor concentration and judgment.

The best way to confront your fears is to educate yourself about them. Research how you can protect yourself from your fears, but also learn the reality of your fears. Many fears actually have no basis in reality! For example, many people are terrified to fly; however, according to the National Transportation Safety Board, the odds of dying in a plane crash are about 8.5 million to 1. On the flip side, being injured in a motorcycle accident is far more likely, so you should take precautions, such as always wearing a helmet and proper clothing.

Learning about your fears will help you become firmly grounded in what is likely to occur rather than what you are afraid will occur. After doing this, you will be better educated about your fears and able to cope with them appropriately.

Write down your 3 biggest fears. Describe why you are afraid of these things.

1.

2.

3.

Research these 3 fears. Now write down the reality of your fears. When you feel scared, refer back to this page.

1.

2.

3.

How did this exercise help you? Were you able to put any of your fears to rest?

Confront your fears.

Writer Henry S. Haskins thought of fear in the following way: "Panic at the thought of doing a thing is a challenge to do it." Turn your greatest fear on its head by confronting it. When you seek out what you are afraid of, you are taking back the power from fear.

For example, if you feel anxious and fearful in crowded public places (as do 1 in 5 Americans, according to the National Institute of Mental Health), purposely seek out a crowd and become part of it. If you fear the dentist (as do 58 percent of Americans), schedule an appointment with your dentist to have him or her explain what goes on during a check-up. Those who are afraid of flying (1 in 3 Americans) may schedule a tour of a plane or talk to a pilot.

Confronting your fears will demystify them, allowing them to be conquered. As feminist and author Margaret Atwood famously said, "This above all, to refuse to be a victim."

Have you ever attempted to confront one of your fears before? If so, what did you do? What was the result?

Choose one major fear. Create a plan of action for how you will confront this fear. What steps will you take?

Do you feel you were successful at addressing your fear? Why or why not?

Record your accomplishments to silence your inner critic.

Although some of your life goals may not be accomplished, it is likely you have many achievements already under your belt. Relive your successes. Your accomplishments up to this point are an important part of your life's direction.

The first step to becoming immune to the criticisms of others is to silence the critic within yourself. As an African proverb states, "When there is no enemy within, the enemies outside cannot hurt you." Counteract nasty self-talk with reassuring, productive thoughts. Keep a running tally of your accomplishments to banish self-criticism — everything from praise you received at work to a delicious new dinner you cooked.

Even the seemingly small things are relevant, and what you make of your accomplishments is what matters. For instance, if you try ice skating, you can be happy that you were able to go around the rink twice, or you can be unhappy because you were *only* able to go around the rink twice. The choice is yours.

Do you feel like an accomplished individual? Does negative self-talk sometimes make you feel less accomplished than you actually are?

Make a list of some of your most important accomplishments here. Later, expand this list and continue to update it.

Write down one example of negative self-talk and combat it with a positive, productive statement.

Change your daily routine.

When your routine is the same day in and day out, you may start to feel unhappy, bored, or listless. People often carry out their daily routine without a thought. Stop sleepwalking through your day! Change your daily routine, and you will reinvigorate your life.

This can be as simple as driving a new route to work, trying an exotic food, or rock climbing instead of running at the gym. Mixing up your routine is a great start toward challenging yourself, building confidence, breaking out of a rut, and discovering new adventures.

As Lewis Carroll's Alice in Wonderland says, "I know who I was when I got up this morning, but I think I must have been changed several times since then." You will be amazed at how reenergized you feel after making even a small adjustment to your daily routine.

Describe your daily routine; include all habitual tasks or activities you do daily.

Brainstorm ways you can mix up your daily routine. For instance, you might walk your dog along a new route.

What were the benefits of changing your daily routine?

Explore your spirituality.

Spirituality can add a dimension to your life that brings happiness, peace, and an overall sense of well-being. Studies have shown that people with some sense of spirituality have less hypertension, less stress, less depression, and are better able to cope with life — especially during difficult times.

Spirituality doesn't have to mean adhering to a specific religious faith, although it can if you choose. When you explore spirituality, faith, prayer, and trust in a higher power, you will surely find a few aspects that enrich your life.

If you do practice a specific faith — from Buddhism to Judaism — you will find that religious practices bond you to a group that is acting on the same principles, creating a sense of community and belonging.

Incorporating certain traditions and aspects of spirituality can truly enrich your daily life. Feeling connected to a higher power can be extremely comforting and uplifting, so explore and see what might interest you.

How do you currently incorporate spirituality in your life? Do you practice a certain religion? Do you pray?

Prayer can have amazing benefits — and you don't have to adhere to any religion to enjoy the rewards. Take just a few minutes to sit quietly and ask for guidance, understanding, or clarity about any situation in your life — from a difficult coworker to illness to a relationship problem. Explain the issue you are having below, then see how quiet thoughts can bring you comfort.

How did incorporating spirituality affect your emotions, stress level, and sense of well-being? Reflect on your experience.

Rediscover your city!

Do you want a fun way to reconnect with friends or just get reenergized? Pretend to be a tourist in your own town.

People often take their city from granted after living there for some time. You will feel rejuvenated if you remind yourself why you love your city. Does it have amazing cafés and restaurants? Is the nightlife unbeatable? Are there interesting museums or exhibits? Is there a special event in town? Rediscover the niches, culture, and hidden gems that you may have forgotten or overlooked.

Go online and download a list of the 50 top things to see and do in your city. Or, buy a guidebook, check the entertainment section of your local newspaper, or head out to a restaurant or play that was reviewed on the radio. Take a bike tour, see a concert, visit the zoo, or check out a local landmark. Stop by a festival that comes to town. Take pictures and buy souvenirs. You will feel reinvigorated by your city and your time spent with friends exploring a fascinating place — your home!

Rediscovering your city will get you excited about where you live and help you find new activities you can enjoy.

What are your favorite activities or places to visit in your city?

_____

_____

_____

_____

_____

_____

Come up with a list of things you can do to rediscover your city. For example, maybe there is a museum you have always wanted to visit. Check off each activity as you do it.

❑ _____

❑ _____

❑ _____

❑ _____

❑ _____

❑ _____

❑ _____

❑ _____

❑ _____

What did you discover about your city? Did you uncover anything new, interesting, or fun you didn't know about?

_____

_____

_____

_____

_____

Join a gym.

Joining a gym can greatly contribute to a happier, healthier life. Not only are you able to work out and get in shape, but you are surrounded by countless opportunities to meet new people.

When you become more active you are likely to make friends who share your interest in exercise and fitness. This can help keep you motivated to exercise, and, with your newfound self-confidence, you are also more likely to strike up a conversation and pursue new opportunities for socializing. This will result in an improvement in your overall quality of life.

There are many kinds of gyms, offering a variety of amenities, classes, and programs. You can use Websites like www.healthclubdirectory. com to find gyms and health clubs in your local area. Choose one that is right for you, and enjoy the health and social benefits.

Do you currently or have you ever had a membership to a gym? What were the benefits? Were there any drawbacks?

Research a few local gyms or health clubs. Write down the name of the facility, as well as the pros and cons of each location.

Gym 1:

Pros:

Cons:

Gym 2:

Pros:

Cons:

Gym 3:

Pros:

Cons:

Which gym did you choose? Have you met any new people? What do you like most about your membership?

42

Get a pet, stress less.

Studies have shown that people who have regular interaction with pets are happier and healthier. The Centers for Disease Control reports that having pets can lower your blood pressure, cholesterol, and reduce feelings of loneliness by increasing opportunities for exercise, outdoor activities, and socialization.

Just try not to smile when you are greeted by a loving pet whose entire life revolves around you, even after you have been fighting traffic for an hour. A recent study showed that stockbrokers in New York who had dogs or cats as pets had lower blood pressure than those who did not.

Finally, adding a pet to your home ensures that you will always have company, and having a family pet promotes bonding and a sense of responsibility in children. Even if it is just a simple goldfish in a bowl! So get a dog, cat, fish, bird, or other pet to further enjoy life.

At the very least, try spending some quality time with a friend's or neighbor's animal. You will reap the many benefits loving pets bring!

Think back to your very first pet. Recall how caring for and bonding with that animal made you feel. What is your favorite memory of that pet?

_____

_____

_____

_____

_____

_____

Write down your thoughts on getting a pet, including which kind you would like. If you already have a pet, consider how you might spend more time with your pet to further reap the benefits to your health and happiness.

_____

_____

_____

_____

_____

_____

Which benefits have spending time with a pet offered you?

- ❏ Companionship
- ❏ Opportunities for exercise
- ❏ Opportunities to meet other pet owners
- ❏ Compassion
- ❏ Relaxation
- ❏ Responsibility
- ❏ Laughter

Dance to your favorite song.

Grab a few minutes in the evening to dance to your favorite song — Mayo Clinic researchers have concluded that dancing reduces stress, increases energy, improves strength, and increases coordination! Taking time to move your body when no one is watching frees you from feeling self-conscious and is great exercise.

Studies have also shown that music has many health and mood benefits. Listening to your favorite song makes you cheerful and puts you in a more optimistic state of mind. Music also fuels creativity and effectively relieves stress.

Letting go and dancing freely to your favorite song is a great way to boost your mood and improve your health — in just a few short minutes!

How do you feel when you hear some of your favorite music?

Make a list of ways you can better incorporate music and movement into your life.

Reflect on the ways in which music and movement have improved your mood or reduced stress levels.

Try a new recipe.

Cooking can be a relaxing way to wind down at the end of the day. Cooking for your significant other, or even just for yourself, can be interesting and fun if you try out new recipes.

Cooking at home also benefits your health. People who cook usually eat smaller portions than they would at a restaurant. A recent study showed that people consume 50 percent more calories, fat and sodium when they eat out than when they cook at home.

In addition, when you cook, you can control what goes into each dish—a big benefit when you consider many restaurant meals are prepared with unhealthy oils, butter, and creamy sauces. Try recipes that include fruits, vegetables, and whole grains.

Finally, you should always make dining a pleasant experience. Use a nice placemat and a cloth napkin. Sip a glass of wine or sparkling water with dinner. Set a relaxing mood by lighting candles and playing music. Savor each bite and take your time. Enjoy your meal and your great company.

How often do you make meals at home for yourself or your family? Would you like to cook at home more often?

Jot down a recipe you would like to try. Make a list of the ingredients you will need to shop for.

How did you enjoy trying this new recipe? What did you like about cooking at home?

Find a hobby that relaxes you and indulge in it.

Make time each week for a hobby that you find relaxing. Hobbies have been medically proven to reduce stress and increase happiness. In one study, published in the *Journal of the American Medical Association*, female heart patients reported significant decreases in heart rate and blood pressure while working on a simple craft project.

For instance, take a pottery or painting class — you will likely find it satisfying to produce something beautiful with your own hands that you can be proud of. Or, you might take up a physical hobby, such as fly-fishing or gardening. It will feel great to do something active and be in the fresh air.

Improved health is just one example of the many positive benefits a hobby will bring to your life. Someone who has their own hobbies, projects, and interests has a more enriched life. This person tends to be more self-confident, interesting, and well-rounded than others. So find a hobby you can commit to and enjoy it.

Do you currently have any hobbies?

List the hobbies you would find relaxing.

Have you tried any of the hobbies on your list? What have you enjoyed?

Clear clutter by donating to the less-fortunate.

Do you have extra kitchen appliances, clothes you no longer wear, or a TV sitting in your garage? Give your rooms and closets a spring cleaning, then donate your extra things to homeless shelters and thrift stores. Stores like Goodwill get donations from more than 65 million people each year!

Make piles for clothes, shoes, toys, furniture, housewares, and other items to give away. Ask yourself these questions when trying to decide whether to keep an object or donate it: Do I need it? Does it make me happy? Have I used it in the last year? If you answer "no" to any of these questions, give it away.

Even if the item feels small or trivial, donate it rather than throwing it away. People in need will appreciate the things you donate, and your home will be free of clutter.

Experience what author Maya Angelou meant when she said, "I have found that among its other benefits, giving liberates the soul of the giver." Truly, when you donate to make your home more clean and organized, you will feel anxiety lifting off you.

Do you feel weighed down by clutter around your home?

What do you know you can give away? Where do you plan to donate?

Describe the feeling of donating and unloading your clutter.

Recognize when a professional can help.

If you are struggling with a difficult past, divorce, loss of a loved one, grief, depression, anger, or any other issues, you should consider seeking professional therapy, counseling, or medical care. There is never any shame in recognizing when a problem becomes too big for you to handle alone.

The American Psychiatric Association believes that with proper professional diagnosis and treatment, the vast majority of issues can be overcome. Consulting a professional can help you find the root of the problem and get proper medications or treatment options, as well as peace of mind.

Never let sadness, resentment, or anger spiral out of control. It takes courage to be willing to look into a painful past or confront difficult and scary issues; however, recognizing when to reach beyond yourself and the love of family and friends to get the guidance you need will help you come back to a place of happiness and peace.

Have you ever sought professional counseling or medical help for a difficult issue? How did it help or affect you?

Describe a difficult issue you struggle with. Do you think you would consider seeking professional help?

Describe your goals for coping with your issue or concern. What do you hope to accomplish?

Eliminate one thing in your life that brings you down.

To be truly happy, sometimes you must eliminate unhealthy people and situations from your life.

For instance, you might feel stuck in a dead-end job. Resolve to take the first step toward finding a new one. Or, perhaps there is a person in your life who constantly brings you down. Interestingly, a recent survey showed that almost half (48 percent) of women admitted to having a toxic friend who has prevented them from spending time with the people they truly care about.

If there is someone or something in your life that isn't making you happy, stop wasting your time! As Charles Darwin said, "A man who dares to waste one hour of time has not discovered the value of life."

It may take some courage to eliminate this stuff from your life, but you will feel much more fulfilled once you are able to concentrate on the people and things that do make you happy.

Is there a situation or person in your life that is toxic to your happiness or health? Imagine your life without this situation or person — how would you feel?

Devise a plan to remove this situation or person from your life. What steps must you take?

Reflect on eliminating this situation or person. How did it go? Were you nervous or afraid? How do you feel now that you have one less downer in your life?

Practice yoga to strengthen your body and mind.

Yoga has gotten really popular with celebrities and world-class athletes, and that's because it is an amazing workout with tons of benefits.

Doing yoga regularly gives you long, lean muscles; increases flexibility; reduces stress; increases stamina and energy; improves balance; prevents injury; and improves posture. In a yoga session, you will hold various postures — called asanas — while focusing on breathing, balance, alignment, and different muscle groups. The result is a toned, defined body and increased focus. Even The American Council on Exercise concluded that yoga is "a valuable addition to any exercise routine, offering factors often neglected in traditional workouts."

Yoga classes are available at gyms and private studios and are offered for every age and skill level, so find a class in your area. There's a reason yoga has been around for more than 3,000 years — it offers calm and focus to strengthen your body and mind.

Have you ever tried yoga in the past? What did you think of it?

Check off the ways you feel you could benefit from yoga:

- ❑ Flexibility
- ❑ Strengthen and lengthen muscles
- ❑ Better posture
- ❑ Lessened back pain
- ❑ Relaxation
- ❑ Mental focus
- ❑ Stamina
- ❑ Better balance for other physical activities
- ❑ Bounce back faster from injuries
- ❑ Variation in your workout program

Reflect on your experience with yoga. Describe the mental and physical benefits. Is this something you will continue?

Make a master list and divide household responsibilities.

Household responsibilities can be a real pain if not everyone is doing their share. Make a master list of all the tasks that keep your household running smoothly, such as cooking, cleaning, transportation, childcare, maintenance, and bill paying. Make a spreadsheet with categories for daily, weekly, monthly, and bimonthly chores, then divide the list among your family members or roommates. Hang the spreadsheet in a place where everyone can see it, such as in the kitchen.

Dividing chores is a test of both respect and compromise. Everyone should be dedicated to harmony in the home; thus, you must hold household members accountable to completing their chores. If you have young children, provide some incentive by planning fun activities, outings, or even prizes for those who complete their chores on time.

Eliminating conflict over household chores will make life at your house much happier.

An imbalanced division of labor can cause major issues in a household. What problems have you encountered when household duties were lopsided?

- ❑ Resentment
- ❑ Frustration
- ❑ Feelings of being overwhelmed
- ❑ Anger
- ❑ Arguing or bickering
- ❑ Feeling disrespected
- ❑ Complaining
- ❑ Shouting or yelling
- ❑ Passive-aggressive behavior, such as leaving dirty dishes in the sink until the person cleans them
- ❑ A messy household

Are there chores you don't mind, can tolerate, or actually enjoy? Write them here, and volunteer to take on these responsibilities in your household.

How did creating a master list benefit the peace and harmony in your household? How did the members of your household react?

SECRET 51

Invoke your creative side.

Just like your other muscles, the creative side of your brain needs to be exercised regularly. Start invoking your creative side by taking in art and culture. Visit a museum, take in an art exhibit, or see a ballet or opera.

You may not consider yourself an especially creative or artistic person, but that should never stop you. Don't think you must be an expert in African dance to enjoy a performance of this type. You need not know a thing about Mozart to appreciate and enjoy listening to his music. Everyone has a unique imagination and perspective on life that should be demonstrated through creativity.

As activist and author Mary Lou Cook said, "Creativity is inventing, experimenting, growing, taking risks, breaking rules, making mistakes, and having fun." So, don't be afraid to paint, draw, write, compose music, dance, or express your creativity in any way that moves you.

Do you consider yourself a creative person? What was the last creative thing you did?

Draw, sketch, or color a picture of something that inspires you creatively.

How did you feel creating this image? Does being creative make you feel liberated, excited, relaxed, self-conscious, etc.?

Eliminate toxic social scenes or people.

Just as chemicals are toxic to your body, certain people or social scenes are toxic to your happiness and well-being.

Is there someone in your social circle who makes you feel uneasy? Do you have a friend who brings out the worst in you? Perhaps you find that hanging out with a particular circle of friends places you in precarious situations. If so, it is time to find a new social circle.

Only you can determine what social scenes are healthy for you. But ask yourself, "Is this person or situation contributing to my well-being?" "Would my partner be happy if he or she was here?" "Do I feel good about myself after spending time with this person or group?" If not, remove yourself from those situations.

While it may be difficult, it is beneficial to your happiness to step away from those friendships or social scenes and find new, healthy ones.

Is there a person in your social life who is toxic to your happiness and well-being? How do you feel after spending time with him or her?

Brainstorm how you can prevent this friendship from negatively affecting your life. How can you say no before you wind up in a precarious situation?

Describe the experience. Was it difficult? Did you feel guilty?

Establish a diverse group of friends.

All great friends will boost your happiness and well-being but having a diverse social group is especially wonderful.

Oftentimes, people gravitate toward people who are just like them. However, you will expand your knowledge of other cultures and learn to compromise and consider other viewpoints by making friends of different ethnicities, religious backgrounds, political views, and sexual orientation. For example, a recent study from the University of California, Berkeley, found that cross-racial friendships may reduce anxiety in both academic and social situations.

Even though you don't share all the same attitudes or beliefs, your friends should have positive attitudes about relationships, career, and family life. These friends should make you feel like you belong in their group.

So, open yourself up to finding people with different and fresh perspectives. Incorporate diverse, interesting people into your social circle, and it will benefit your mind, attitude, and emotional well-being.

Do you feel you have a diverse group of friends? If so, what are the benefits for you? If not, would you like to diversify?

Qualities and values are what are most important in friends — transcending race, religion, political affiliation, and sexuality. Make a list of the qualities you like your friends to possess.

Have you successfully expanded your social circle to include more diverse people? How has it benefitted you?

Make a scrapbook or photo album to document your life.

To fully embrace life, we must appreciate the lives of those who have gone before us, paved the way for us, and shaped our personalities and attitudes. You and your family and friends have a special story that makes you who you are.

In this spirit, make a scrapbook or album that documents your life and your family's life. Tell the story of your history and countries of origin, and share pictures of loved ones. Make scrapbooks of you and your friends' travels and adventures. Create a keepsake for special events, such as your wedding day, a special party, or the birth of a child. Preserve mementos of the occasion so you can revisit them for years to come.

Documenting your life will bring back a flood of amazing, happy memories and inspire you to make new ones.

What are some special occasions or memorable events you would like to document?

Make a list of the materials you will need to create your scrapbook or album, including things like craft paper or double-sided tape. Then, set aside a few hours to complete your project.

Describe how making your scrapbook or album made you feel. Who will you share it with?

SECRET
55

Create and stick to a budget.

In the 21st century, the majority of American couples are living beyond their means. In 2007 alone, Americans charged $2.2 trillion in purchases and cash advances on major credit cards.

Living beyond your means can threaten the safety of your entire family and can cause major stress. In fact, finances are the number one cause of conflict among married couples.

To keep your sanity and your money, create a budget that tracks both essential and discretionary expenses. Your budget should include items such as household bills, credit obligations, incidentals, discretionary funds, hidden costs, emergency funds, and money for savings or vacations. This way, you will be able to stay out of debt and have a clear picture of your financial future.

Drawing up a budget allows you to evaluate your current spending and make cutbacks or expansions in necessary areas. Sticking to it will keep you happy, relaxed, and worry-free.

Are you a natural saver or spender? Do you have money saved up or are you in debt?

Make a quick list of the top expenses you have on a monthly basis. This will help you when you go to make your complete budget.

What are your goals for saving money or paying down debts? How has creating a budget helped?

Get outside help.

You can eliminate a lot of stress from your life if you aren't afraid to ask for help when you need it. If you are simply too busy for housework, for instance, examine whether your budget permits you to hire outside help. Hiring a cleaning person may be well worth it if it relieves a lot of stress.

If money is tight, look for bartering opportunities. Find friends and neighbors with similar needs. If you and a friend both have young children, alternate babysitting weekly. Or, offer to swap lawn-mowing services with a neighbor. If you come across a home repair project that requires certain equipment or special skills, find a neighbor who is willing to help in exchange for your services at a later date.

If you are too shy to ask for help when you need it, you risk getting burnt out from all your responsibilities. Getting outside help will lighten your load, relieve stress, and preserve your happiness.

How good are you about asking for help when you need it? Are you up-front or shy?

Think of a few situations in your life where you could benefit from getting outside help. Now go and ask!

Describe your experience with asking for help when you need it. Did it relieve stress and prevent you from feeling overwhelmed?

Drink green tea to improve your overall health.

Experts believe that green tea can vastly improve your health and decrease the risk of disease. Green tea is reported to contain the highest concentration of polyphenols, a powerful antioxidant. Antioxidants search for and neutralize free radicals, damaging compounds in the body that cause cell death and alter DNA and cells.

Green tea has been widely used in traditional Asian medicine for centuries and is said to prevent everything from headaches to cancer.

Green tea contains natural caffeine, although it is only about one-third as much as a cup of coffee. So, trade your morning espresso for a cup of iced or hot green tea. Also, try different varieties infused with lemon, ginger, honey, or citrus.

No matter how you drink it, green tea will help you enjoy a healthy boost of energy and numerous physical benefits.

What are your past experiences with green tea?

_____

_____

_____

_____

_____

_____

The following are some of the many benefits of green tea. Check off those that appeal to you.

❑ Lessened risk of cancer
❑ Suppressed appetite
❑ Increased metabolism
❑ Less inflammation
❑ Lower blood pressure
❑ Better memory
❑ Lower risk of arthritis
❑ Lower risk of heart disease
❑ Improved sun protection for the skin
❑ Boost of energy

Reflect on having incorporated green tea into your diet. Do you enjoy it? Do you plan to continue drinking it?

_____

_____

_____

_____

_____

Satisfy your emotional needs with things other than food.

Emotional eating leads to overeating, excess calories, and weight gain. To stay happy and healthy, you should identify the circumstances that cause you to eat out of emotion, rather than hunger.

The 5 typical emotions or states that cause overeating are loneliness, boredom, anger, stress, and fatigue. You might have a bad day at work or go through a tough breakup and turn to food for comfort.

In addition, some people reward themselves with food. However, a celebration should not call for eating an entire pizza.

Learn to recognize this behavior and stop it. Overeating or having an unhealthy meal will only make you feel upset and frustrated.

Find non-food-related ways to satisfy emotional needs. Exercise to relieve stress and vent frustration. Call a friend when you have a tough day. Listen to music to relax you. Or, treat yourself in a way that doesn't include food, such as taking a hot bath or getting a massage.

Are you an emotional eater? What are some situations or emotions that typically cause you to overeat or eat an unhealthy meal?

Think of one situation that leads to emotional eating for you. Now, write a list of things you can do to prevent emotional eating.

Has this exercise helped you recognize emotional eating and stop it before it starts?

Start a food journal.

Most people would be much happier if they lost a few pounds and ate healthier. The best way to lose weight is to keep track of what you eat and drink throughout the day in a food journal.

By logging what you eat and drink, you hold yourself accountable for every soda and bag of chips, which can quickly add up to extra calories. Not even a bite of a cookie will sneak by.

You can use a basic blank notebook to record your daily intake, or you might want to buy a diet journal, which provides space to record physical fitness activities, supplements, energy levels, and weekly goals.

Start each day of your food journal by recording your weight. Then write down everything you eat and drink throughout the day. Last, calculate your total weight loss at the end of each week! You will be amazed at how much easier it is to lose weight with a food journal.

Do you know how many calories you consume each day? Have you ever kept a food journal before?

Write down your goals for using a food journal. For example, how many calories would you like to consume daily? How much weight would you like to lose?

Elaborate on your experience using the food journal. Has it proven helpful? Have you successfully trimmed down or learned to eat a more balanced diet?

Personalize your workspace.

Given the amount of time you spend at work, you will be happier if your workspace is a place you enjoy. Also, you will be able to do better work if your cubicle, desk, or office is clean, organized, and feels more personal.

While you don't want to clutter your desk, your day will be brighter if you customize your workspace with items that show your personality. Put up a few photos of your friends and family. Hang a calendar that shows one of your interests, like dogs or beautiful beaches. Bring in a special coffee mug from home. Get a plant. Display a rock garden. Or, use a colorful cup as a pencil holder.

Your personalized workspace will make you smile and may even invite friendly inquiries from coworkers. Even if you work from home, you can keep your desk personal and inspiring. And your employer will thank you when your productivity increases!

Describe your current workspace and work environment.

Make a list of things you might do or bring in to make your workspace more personal.

Are you comfortable in your personalized workspace? Has personalizing your workspace had any positive effects on your workday?

Break large jobs into small, manageable tasks.

At times it is hard to stay confident when a giant task is looming over you. Before beginning, break the job down into smaller, more manageable parts. Business tycoon Warren Buffett once said, "I don't look to jump over 7-foot bars; I look around for 1-foot bars that I can step over." He meant that he sought out realistic, manageable milestones before tackling a larger goal.

For instance, if every corner of your house is an unsightly mess, deal with each room one at a time. If you have been asked to make Thanksgiving dinner, break the meal up into courses and tackle the dishes one by one.

Always acknowledge when you have accomplished a task by crossing it off a larger list. Tackling smaller components of a larger goal will keep you feeling motivated, which positively impacts your overall outlook and chance of success.

Do you set realistic goals for yourself, or do you bite off more than you can chew?

Choose one of your larger goals. Now, make a list of smaller components you can begin with to work toward that goal.

Reflect on your success with breaking down a larger task in manageable parts. Were you able to complete the larger task more easily or efficiently?

Act like a kid again.

As children, we were all more open to the moment, delighted by new things, and less self-conscious. We were quick to laugh and play alongside anyone and explore uncharted territory without hesitation.

To revisit the wonder of a child's carefree lifestyle, spend some time acting like a kid again. Be playful at home: Put on music and dance around, dust off that Frisbee, or play a board game. Visit the zoo or an amusement park. Fingerpaint. The key is to do something silly and fun and not to take life too seriously.

Even as far back as the 13th century, St. Thomas Aquinas knew: "It is requisite for the relaxation of the mind that we make use, from time to time, of playful deeds and jokes."

Acting like a kid again, no matter your age, is a great way to enjoy life without stress or fear.

Are you playful, or do you consider yourself more serious?

Make a list of some of the childhood games or activities you enjoyed that you might take up again.

How has acting like a kid again helped you better enjoy life?

Write a list of regrets, then throw it away.

How often have you lamented, "If only I had done that," or "If only that had happened to me"? Author Mercedes Lackay has written, "If only. Those must be the two saddest words in the world." Indeed, regret is possibly the most useless emotion because it holds us prisoner to what cannot be undone.

Let go of these feelings by writing a list of everything you regret in your life. Then, take the paper and crumple it into a ball or tear it to shreds. Throw the paper away. This physical act symbolizes eliminating remorse and regret from your life. You have now given yourself permission to be let off the hook for your missteps and missed opportunities.

The best you can do is take a lesson from each situation, then see the future with a happy, positive outlook. Today is the perfect day to take a risk or go after a dream! As George Eliot wrote, "It is never too late to become what you might have been."

Describe how you feel when you think about regrets. Do you feel weighed down? Bitter? Unable to forgive?

Next, write your list of regrets on another piece of paper, crumple it or tear it, and throw it away. Describe how that exercise felt in the moment.

Reflect on how you feel now that you have completed the exercise of making a list of your regrets and throwing it away. Do you feel this symbolic act has helped you let go?

Create a list of goals for the coming month.

To jumpstart a newfound feeling of accomplishment, create a list of goals for the next 30 days. These should be things you can complete on a daily or weekly basis, such as getting your oil changed, reading a good book, or cleaning out the garage. Hang your list in a highly visible place like the bathroom mirror or the refrigerator.

Reviewing this list often will remind you of the things that are important to you. In turn, this will make you work on the steps that will help you achieve these goals. For example, if one of your goals is to read a new book this month, then the steps you would take might include setting aside an hour each night to read.

Cross items off your list as you do them. This will give you an immediate sense of satisfaction and keep you motivated toward the next item on your list. Setting achievable goals for a set amount of time will help you feel happy and accomplished.

Some people are habitual list-makers. Do you often make to-do lists or chart your goals? Do you think it can or will help you meet your goals?

Write a preliminary list of goals for the next 30 days. Later, transfer this list to a piece of paper you hang in a highly visible place. Repeat this exercise every month.

Were you able to meet all or most of your goals? How did it feel to check off each task as you completed it?

Stop relying on other people for your happiness.

Actress Lucille Ball once said, "Love yourself first and everything else falls into line. You really have to love yourself to get anything done in this world." What she meant was that you cannot rely on others for your happiness. You are not one-half of a person, looking for another half to complete you. You are responsible for your own joy.

Thus, never enter into a relationship or friendship thinking it is going to become the sole source of your happiness. Your happiness is simply not something that others can provide. Relationships should enhance your joy, not serve as its only source.

Remember, enjoying life is about nurturing the relationship you have with yourself. Find activities that you are passionate about, make friends who enrich your life, and always create time for yourself. You will find that your life is filled with pleasure, without turning to anyone or anything else for your joy.

Write about a time when you mistakenly relied on another person for happiness. What did you take from this experience?

_____

_____

_____

_____

Come up with a list of 10 things you can do to nurture your relationship with yourself.

1. _____

2. _____

3. _____

4. _____

5. _____

6. _____

7. _____

8. _____

9. _____

10. _____

Reflect on your success with not relying on others for your happiness. How have you learned to better love yourself as an individual?

_____

_____

_____

_____

Celebrate your uniqueness.

Each of us has features that make us unique — although we may mistakenly view them as flaws. Often, we feel desire or even pressure to fit in; however, you can't truly enjoy life and be happy until you learn to celebrate your unique qualities and traits.

As German writer Johann Wolfgang von Goethe said, "Certain flaws are necessary for the whole. It would seem strange if old friends lacked certain quirks." Truly, what you may see as flaws are really only quirks that make you interesting and unique. A loud laugh, gap between your teeth, or bumpy nose are often what make you *you*. Over time, people usually discover that their unique features are what they love most about themselves.

You will be much happier once you own your size, shape, and features with pride instead of trying to be someone different. Embrace your unique look and style!

What feature or features have you always viewed as flaws? How has this affected your happiness?

What quirky or interesting features of yours do you like or appreciate?

Are there any features you once viewed as flaws that you are now beginning to accept or embrace? How can you better accept your unique features?

Make your bedroom a sanctuary.

Your bedroom is a place for rest, relaxation, and intimacy, so treat it as such. Decorate using cool, relaxing colors such as blues, purples, and greens. Hang pictures of whatever relaxes you or reminds you of happy times — pictures from your wedding day, a favorite trip, images of family and friends, or vistas of natural beauty.

Clear out clutter and remove unnecessary distractions. Watch TV in another room. Keep items that heighten your stress levels — such as bills, work, exercise machines, or medical items — in a separate part of the house.

Make your room comfortable. Invest in luxurious sheets and a soft comforter. Buy a small CD player and listen to relaxing music. Arrange lightly scented candles (strong smells can interfere with sleep) around your room to create a peaceful atmosphere.

When your bedroom is a sanctuary, you will sleep better and wake up feeling revived and energized.

Describe your bedroom. What colors do you have in the room, what is on the walls? Is the room cluttered or neat?

_____

_____

_____

_____

Check off the ways you can make your bedroom a sanctuary to improve your sleep and mood.

- ❏ Hang pictures of peaceful scenes
- ❏ Remove TV
- ❏ Remove bills and paperwork
- ❏ Buy high-thread-count sheets
- ❏ Get a soft comforter
- ❏ Arrange candles
- ❏ Play relaxing music
- ❏ Decorate using cool colors
- ❏ Hang flowing curtains to keep out light
- ❏ Arrange books neatly on a bookshelf
- ❏ Eliminate clutter

What have you done to create a peaceful sanctuary in your bedroom? How have these changes affected your sleep, energy level, and mood?

_____

_____

_____

_____

_____

Leave work at the office.

Writer Margaret Fuller once noted, "Men for the sake of getting a living forget to live." If you find yourself devoting inordinate chunks of time to work, or bringing stress from work home with you, ask yourself how it is affecting your relationships. You are probably neglecting friends, pets, and family — or yourself!

The world is not likely to fall apart if you do not return a phone call immediately, so it makes no sense to add such stress to your life. Refrain from working more than 9 hours a day, and take at least 1 day a week to not work at all.

Instead of working yourself to the point of exhaustion every day, or bringing extra work home with you, make sure the hours you spend at the office are quality ones. Then, spend your time off with the people you love.

How often do you bring work home or come home stressed from work? How do you think this affects your relationships?

Check off the ways you can leave work and work-related stress at the office to better enjoy your life.

- ❑ Use your commute home to unwind. Listen to music, clear your head, and release pent-up stress.
- ❑ Make plans with your loved ones for after work. Cook dinner, play a board game, or go to a movie.
- ❑ Disconnect from your email and turn off your cell phone when you get home.
- ❑ Agree to vent or talk about work for only 20 minutes after you get home. Then, leave it in the past.
- ❑ Talk to your partner, roommate, or kids about their day, instead of focusing on your workday.
- ❑ Exercise or go for a walk after work to relieve stress.
- ❑ Finish more work by getting to the office a bit early, while your loved ones sleep.

How have you seen your relationships improve as a result of leaving work at the office?

SECRET 69

Plan a getaway!

According to a study by the travel company Expedia, American workers collectively give back 175 million paid vacation days to their employers every year. You work hard — so enjoy your vacation days!

Getting away doesn't have to take lots of money or time — a night spent in a local bed and breakfast, or a weekend devoted to exploring a nearby destination can be just as significant as an exotic beach vacation.

Whatever you do, the health benefits are extensive. Studies have shown that people who take yearly vacations have better mental health, sleep better, are more productive, have less anxiety, and even live longer!

Better still, an escape can reignite your love life. Taking a vacation is a perfect way to inspire romance and reconnect with a loved one.

A change of scenery is always rejuvenating, so plan an escape today. The important thing is to get away and enjoy a little time off.

Describe the last getaway you had. Where did you go, what activities did you do? How did you feel upon return?

Make a list of getaways you can take in the coming months that will help you relax and refresh.

Reflect on the getaway you took. How did the change of scenery energize or invigorate you?

Turn off the TV and do a hands-on activity.

Openness, flexibility, and creativity are keys to enjoying a hearty, healthy social life. Start by turning off the television. Watching a sitcom or movie can be relaxing, but it won't help you enjoy life to the fullest.

Instead of sedentary activities like watching TV, choose hands-on activities that will expand your cultural horizons or help you find new creative interests. Consider volunteering, taking cooking classes, joining a political organization, attending wine-tasting events, getting a membership at a museum, joining an improv comedy group, signing up for art classes — even karaoke counts as a creative endeavor.

By participating in a hands-on activity, you will do something active and fun while meeting new people with similar interests.

What are your current hands-on interests?

List the hands-on activities you might like to get involved in to be active and cultivate your social life.

What new activities did you try? What did you enjoy? What will you continue to participate in?

Treat yourself to a massage.

Enjoying life has a lot to do with doing something nice for *you* once in a while. So treat yourself to a relaxing indulgence — a massage!

Massage therapy helps to relieve tension headaches, eye strain, back pain, muscle tension, and stiffness by increasing oxygen circulation throughout the body up to 5 times its normal flow. Massage also promotes deep mental relaxation. You might even fall asleep!

You may consider a massage a luxury purchase — one can cost between $55 and $125 — but just think how many times you have spent more than that in a store and have still come home feeling sad and stressed? However, massages do not have to be expensive. Many massage schools offer discounted services so their students can practice their skills. Or, ask a friend or partner to exchange massages.

While massages are wonderful for mental and physical well-being, massages may not be your thing. If that is the case, try indulging in another relaxing activity to reduce stress, such as a daytime nap or a long, hot bath.

Have you ever had a full-body massage in the past? What was your experience? How did you feel afterward?

How would you like to benefit from getting a massage?

- ❑ Relaxation
- ❑ Reduced tension and anxiety
- ❑ Lessened back pain
- ❑ Lessened muscle stiffness
- ❑ Fewer headaches
- ❑ Less eye strain
- ❑ Faster recovery from injury
- ❑ Increased range of motion
- ❑ Lower blood pressure
- ❑ Stronger immune system
- ❑ Improved mental focus post-massage
- ❑ An enjoyable hour!

Reflect on your massage. How did it feel to pamper yourself? How did the massage benefit your mental and physical well-being?

Inspire romance!

With so much to do every day, most people feel more tired than romantic by the end of the day. However, romantic gestures need not require extensive planning or cost a fortune. Indeed, real romance is all about small, intimate moments shared by you and your partner that keep your love life fresh and fulfilling.

Opportunities for romance are all around you, so take advantage of them! Wear a beautiful dress or a button-down shirt and slacks. Dressing up will make your partner feel special that you took the extra time to look nice. This goes for the bedroom as well; now and then, skip the dowdy nightshirt and wear something more exciting to bed. Taking time with your appearance inspires romance and shows your partner you care.

Or, treat your partner like a king or queen for a day. Serve breakfast in bed, give a relaxing massage, or run a hot bath. Let your partner choose a nice restaurant for dinner, or order from a favorite take-out spot and eat by candlelight.

Inspiring romance will invigorate your love life and allow you to bond and connect with your partner.

How romantic are you? What is the most romantic thing you have ever done for someone?

Create a list of ways you can inspire romance in your life. Remember — romance doesn't have to be expensive or very detailed. Just simple, thoughtful gestures will do.

How has being more romantic helped you enjoy life better? Have you felt a new spark in your love life?

Embrace the power of touch.

Reach out to the special people in your life — literally. Touch makes you feel physically and emotionally close to others. In fact, when you hug or hold someone, your body releases a "feel-good" hormone called oxytocin, which creates bonding and trust between people.

Touching goes a long way toward keeping you happy, healthy, and strong. In fact, researchers at Wilkes University in Pennsylvania found that couples who touch each other and have sex a few times a week have 30 percent higher levels of an antibody called immunoglobulin A, which boosts the immune system. So touch your loved one regularly — that is sure to keep the doctor away.

Don't let physical affection with friends, family, and lovers fall by the wayside as the years go by. You will experience much more love and happiness when you embrace the power of physical touch.

How affectionate are you? About how many of these physical touches do you have a day?

Handshakes:

Hugs:

Kisses:

Cuddling:

Holding hands:

Sex:

How do you feel about touching other people? Are you very comfortable, not comfortable at all, or somewhere in between? Who might you be more affectionate with?

How has your life felt richer and happier as the result of the power of touch?

Take it outside.

Author Ralph Waldo Emerson once wrote, "Live in the sunshine, swim the sea, drink the wild air... ." Indeed, fresh air and natural light will do wonders for elevating your mood.

Studies have consistently shown that just a few minutes of natural sunshine a day boosts a person's intake of vitamin D, which improves mood, lowers blood pressure, and prevents bone loss. Additionally, fresh air promotes better breathing and circulation.

Our busy lives often keep us cooped up in an office, car, or house for hours on end. Break the routine by getting outside where you can be surrounded by Mother Nature. Go for a walk, take a hike or bike ride, or spend an afternoon on the beach.

Fresh air and sunshine are available to you any time, so use them often to improve your day and lift your mood.

How often do you spend time outside during an average week? What do you enjoy about being outdoors?

Take at least 20 minutes several times during the coming week to enjoy fresh air and natural sunlight. Write down a list of activities you will do.

Describe how just 20 minutes of being outdoors helped you better enjoy your day? Did you feel recharged, rejuvenated, relaxed, etc.?

Drink 8 glasses of water to stay hydrated and happy.

Water does more than quench your thirst; it is the most important element in the human body! Water is essential to all your bodily functions — including brain function, digesting food, and producing blood.

The human body is made up of more than 50 percent water, so, to replenish it, you must drink 8 glasses of water daily — more if you exercise or play sports.

Staying hydrated flushes harmful toxins out of your body, gives you more energy, and boosts your metabolism. Also, hydration will give you soft skin and better skin elasticity (no wrinkles!).

Choose water over sugary sodas or juices in order to keep yourself hydrated without taking in unwanted calories. And, if 8 glasses sounds like a lot, know that you can actually "eat" some of your 8 cups of water by snacking on oranges, watermelon, celery, and other fruits and vegetables that are mostly water.

When you look and feel great, you can better enjoy life, so stay hydrated for your health and happiness.

How many cups of water would you say you drink a day? Do you drink enough or not enough water?

How can you get your 8 glasses of water a day?

- ❑ Buy water bottles
- ❑ Carry a refillable container or bottle
- ❑ Eat fruits and vegetables with high water content
- ❑ Add lemon, lime, or orange slices to water
- ❑ Drink naturally carbonated water
- ❑ Add cucumber slices to water
- ❑ Mix water with low-calorie powdered drink mixes
- ❑ Drink flavored water that is low in calories

Did you find it easy or difficult to drink 8 glasses or more of water a day? What benefits did you notice from staying better hydrated?

Disconnect from technology to relieve stress.

Stress is a widespread problem — part of the reason is that people spend their waking hours tied to email, cell phones, computers, and other instruments that keep them constantly connected. These days, you can get everything from TV shows, music, games, sports, and more on your mobile phone. Some people even sleep with their cell phones! And, with the internet accessible almost anywhere, people are spending more time "plugged in" and less time relaxing or with loved ones.

A recent study showed that "heavy internet users" (those who spent more than an hour on the Internet a day, not including work- or school-related time) devoted less time to socializing with their partner, children, and friends. They also showed less interest in outdoor activities and spent less time sleeping, relaxing, or resting.

If this is your lifestyle, you must make time to disconnect from technology and reconnect with yourself and loved ones! Turn off your phone and computer for at least 1 hour a day while you are not working. Shut off your cell phone while you sleep. You will be much more relaxed and peaceful without the constant buzz of technology!

How connected do you stay to technology? What technological devices do you use daily? Do they contribute to your stress?

Monitor your internet usage for a 24-hour period. Below, write down every time and for how long you use the internet for personal reasons. How many hours did you spend online?

Try leaving your cell phone at home for one whole day. How did you feel? Did you feel anxious or more relaxed without it?

SECRET 77

Reach out to a friend in need.

Happiness also comes from reaching out to others in need, be it a best friend, family member, or casual acquaintance. Think about your friends, neighbors, and coworkers — is there someone who may need your help right now? Reach out to this person, and think of what you can do to help their situation or make them smile.

You might cook dinner for a friend with a new baby. Or, if you know a coworker is going through a difficult breakup, invite him to join you for lunch one afternoon. Finally, reaching out could be as simple as stopping by to chat with an elderly neighbor who doesn't get many visitors. Something as easy as a phone call or asking someone how they are doing can help when times are tough.

You just might be the bright spot in someone's otherwise dark or difficult day, which can really make you feel wonderful. As novelist and poet George Eliot wrote, "What do we live for, if it is not to make life less difficult for each other?"

What is the last nice thing you did for someone else for no reason other than to brighten his or her day?

Jot down a few people you might reach out to. Write down what you might do for them.

Reflect on reaching out to someone in need. How did this act make your life fuller and more enjoyable?

Frame your favorite photos and hang them around your house.

Framed photos of family, friends, and happy times will make your home a place the inspires and uplifts you. Hang pictures on the walls or place them on your nightstand so you can revisit them frequently.

Also, whenever you travel, pick up a memento that can be displayed in your home to remind you of your adventure. When you are surrounded by this memorabilia, you will be reminded of all the fun you've had with the great people you know. Filling your home with warm memories makes it a space in which you want to spend your time.

You may want to splurge on custom framing for extra-special photos, but simple, inexpensive wooden frames are beautiful and easy to display in many locations. Whatever you do, just don't let favorite photos get stuck in a drawer or dusty album. You will feel warm and happy when you are surrounded by images of people and memories you love.

How does your home make you feel when you spend time there?

What are some photos or mementos that make you happy that you would like to display or frame?

How did displaying framed pictures around your house change the atmosphere for the better?

Use your influence to help someone else.

There are many ways to use your influence to help others that can give your life a sense of purpose and accomplishment. You might help someone you know, such as passing a qualified friend's résumé along to your boss or helping a coworker find new puppies good homes.

On the other hand, you might help someone who is a total stranger. For example, if you notice a person taking advantage of someone less capable, step in and help. If you see that a merchant is overcharging an elderly person, point out the actual price and help with the transaction. Or, perhaps you see someone having car trouble and are good at working on cars. Stopping to help can make you feel wonderful.

Finally, if you witness real trouble, such as someone being assaulted or mugged, you should use personal discretion before stepping in. However, if you do, you may be the hero that stranger was looking for.

Whatever the case, appropriately intervening on behalf of others will make you feel capable and purposeful.

Have you ever stepped in to help on someone's behalf? Were they a friend, acquaintance, or stranger? What was your motivation?

Describe a time when someone else used their influence to help you and how that felt.

The next time you are able to intervene on another person's behalf, reflect on the experience here.

Eat smaller meals more often to enjoy more energy!

For energy-filled, positive days, eat 6 small meals instead of 3 large ones. Eating smaller, more frequent meals will increase your metabolism and keep insulin levels even throughout the entire day.

While skipping meals may seem like a way to lose weight, it actually slows your metabolism and depletes your energy stores. Plus, waiting too long between meals teaches your body to "save up" fat and shift into starvation mode to conserve energy. This not only makes you feel lethargic but can lead to overeating. And everyone knows how sluggish they feel after eating a huge meal.

Instead of 3 large meals, eat small portions about every 3 hours. Try a midmorning snack of low-fat yogurt, nuts, or fruit and a mid-afternoon snack of whole wheat toast and peanut butter or hummus and vegetables. This will help maintain energy levels all day to keep you going strong.

Describe your average meals for a typical day. Include all meals and snacks you normally have.

Try eating 6 smaller portions every few hours, instead of 3 big meals. Jot down a few ideas about what you can eat for these smaller meals. Try this eating plan for a few days.

What was the result of eating smaller meals more frequently? Did you have more energy? Did you make healthier choices?

Limit your alcohol intake.

Enjoy a glass of wine with dinner or an ice-cold beer at a summer barbecue — but don't overdo it. Not only does alcohol impair your ability to think and function, but it is also prevents your liver from breaking down sugar, which turns into stored fat and leads to a "beer belly" or "wine tire."

Additionally, research has showed that drinking alcohol can lead to overeating and unhealthy eating. A study published in the journal *Alcoholism: Clinical and Experimental Research* showed that alcohol triggers cravings for large portions of fatty foods.

Although another glass of wine or another beer may feel good at the time, the next day you may feel sluggish or hungover, which will cause you to be unprepared for work and other activities. And remember, alcohol is a depressant, so use it sparingly. Find fun social events that don't include alcohol — you'll feel better day to day.

What purpose does drinking alcohol serve for you?

For one week, record the alcoholic beverages you have. Then, write down how you felt.

Monday:

Tuesday:

Wednesday:

Thursday:

Friday:

Saturday:

Sunday:

Based on the week recorded above, what can you conclude? Do you often feel tired or hungover? Does alcohol cause you to overeat? Or do you feel you drink in moderation with few negative consequences?

Create a family tree.

A family tree is like a map of who you are. Creating a history of your ancestry can help you know yourself better, including understanding where you came from, the origin of your name, the family members you resemble, and how your family was affected by historical events. Your family tree can include names, birth and death dates, pictures, and even stories about the people in your family.

You can start by interviewing elderly relatives about their childhoods, memories, and family members. Ask to see any important documents, such as citizenship papers, marriage licenses, or birth certificates. You may be interested to see old photographs, military papers, or any other artifacts that can help you better understand your genealogy.

Piecing together your unique genealogy can be a fascinating and enlightening process of self-discovery. Start creating your family tree today to unlock the secrets of who you are and where you come from.

Have you ever researched any of your genealogy? Do you find learning about your ancestors interesting?

Write down the relatives who you might interview to find out clues to your family history. Who or what events are you most curious about?

Describe your experience with creating your family tree. What interesting facts did you learn about yourself?

SECRET
83

Create a list of long-term goals.

Consider what your long-term goals might be. Do you want to get an advanced degree? Start your own business? Have a family? Own a home? Start a college fund?

Long-term goals can be generally defined as goals to be accomplishment over many years, or even an entire lifetime. These types of goals are ones you should plan precisely for and work diligently toward. And, in turn, the rewards will be great once these goals are met.

If you do not know where you are going, you will never get there. Write down your long-term goals and put them in a highly visible place so that you can revisit them often. Reviewing this list of goals often will remind you of the things that are important to you. In turn, this will make you work on the things that will help you achieve those goals.

As French poet and journalist Anatole France once said, "To accomplish great things, we must not only act, but also dream; not only plan, but also believe."

Have you ever mapped out your long-term goals? Are there any you have already begun working toward?

Write down your long-term goals and the first steps toward meeting each one. Later, copy them onto a clean sheet of paper and hang them in a highly visible location.

How does thinking about your long-term goals make you feel? Scared? Anxious? Excited?

Stop and smell the roses.

In today's world, Americans speed through their lives in a mad dash to accomplish one task after another. We are some of the busiest people in the world, with seemingly endless lists of things that need to be done, phone calls and emails that need to be returned, and errands that need to be run. Traveling this fast makes it easy for the joys in your life to whiz by in a blur.

It is difficult to appreciate what you don't have time to see. Therefore, slow down. Look around you. Take time to appreciate the small and sometimes magical moments of everyday life. Push the pause button on your busy schedule, and spend a concentrated chunk of time appreciating your pets, friends, family, interests, and hobbies. Enjoy the small pleasures of your daily life, such as a home-cooked meal, afternoon nap, or a favorite song coming on the radio.

Slowing down allows you to realize how thankful you are for the small wonders of life. You can only enjoy life to the fullest by appreciating the beauty and good around you.

What do you feel like passes you by due to your busy schedule? What might you like to appreciate more?

Spend one day recording all the small pleasures in life that you notice when you slow down.

What was the most significant or wonderful thing you discovered when you slowed down? Did you find you were better able to enjoy life?

SECRET
85

Seek meaningful interactions with friends.

Our fast-paced society sometimes makes it hard to find time for meaningful interactions with people. It is easy to dash off a quick email, leave a voicemail, or text a message and then feel like you have made the effort to connect. But these superficial communications are no substitute for true interaction.

In order to develop real friendships, you must put time and energy into nurturing them. When we are small children, we learn how to play and interact with other children, which plays a major role in both cognitive and social development. Without investing time in others, humans cannot develop correctly.

So, to create special friendships, you must create meaningful time together. Meet a friend for coffee, lunch, a shopping trip, or a round of golf. Send him or her a handwritten birthday card in the mail. Call to say you are thinking of someone, with no occasion at all. Going these extra lengths will endear you to the people you care about most.

Are you guilty of sending a quick message or email and feeling satisfied with your investment in friends?

Jot down a few ideas about how you can better connect with specific friends. Indicate who each person is and how you would like to invest more meaningful time in him or her.

Have you found your friendships more rewarding since seeking out more meaningful interactions with others?

Strive for competition-free friendships.

Jealousy and competition are the great friendship destroyers. There may be reasons to admire or even envy a friend, but succumbing to jealousy or competitiveness will create distance in your relationship. Coveting your friend's high-paying job or attentive partner will shrink your capacity to love and support that friend.

The world is competitive enough without having to compete with your good friends. So, strive to be happy with what you have, and support your friends wholeheartedly so that they will want to support you when good fortune comes your way.

When you are happy with your own life, you won't feel the need to be competitive or jealous with friends. Don't let your pride or ego cause you unnecessary frustration. You should always be a cheerleader for your friends, not a competitor.

Is there a friend you feel competitive with or jealous of? Over what sorts of things?

Make a list of all the things you appreciate and cherish about the friend you mentioned above. This exercise will help you move past jealousy by reminding you of why this friendship is wonderful to you.

How has this exercise helped you recognize and fix the unhealthy competition within your friendship?

Eat a balanced diet to feel great.

Eating a healthy diet does wonders for both your energy and mood. In the age of fast-food restaurants on every corner, consciously eating a balanced diet is more important than ever.

The new dietary guidelines for Americans recommend eating 2 to 3 ounces of lean meat, poultry, or fish. Keep the preparation healthy by baking, broiling, or grilling your meats.

Have at least 5 servings of colorful fruits and veggies, which are packed with nutrients and fiber.

Eat at least 3 ounces of whole grain cereals, bread, crackers, rice, or pasta every day.

Finally, did you realize that some fat is good for you? Just keep your total fat intake between 20 and 35 percent of your daily calories, eating mostly polyunsaturated and monounsaturated fatty acids from fish, nuts, and vegetable oils. Saturated fats should make up less than 10 percent of your calories.

Eating a balanced diet ensures that you get the right nutrients daily, while maintaining a healthy amount of calories.

Do you feel you eat a balanced diet? What food categories would you like to eat more of? Which would you like to eat less of?

Write up an eating plan for your ideal healthy day. Include what you will eat and drink for breakfast, lunch, and dinner, as well as 2 healthy snacks.

How did consciously eating a more balanced diet affect you?

Reevaluate your self-image.

Before you can be truly happy, you must value yourself and craft a positive self-image. Many people are very hard on themselves, comparing themselves to others, resulting in low self-esteem.

Read these questions and answer honestly: Am happy being me? Do I feel like a success? Do I feel valuable to other people? Do I like myself the way I am? Am I happy with my progress as a person?

If you answered no to any of these questions, you need to reevaluate your self-image. Naturally, everyone has things to improve upon, but you should have learned by now that everyone also has many *more* things to be grateful for and proud of!

The power of visualization is incredibly strong, so you should never belittle your accomplishments or wish you were someone else.

See yourself as a loving, growing, learning person and others will feed off your positive self-image.

Draw a picture of how you see yourself. It can be very revealing to describe yourself using an image instead of words.

Describe a few ways you can reevaluate your self-image to see yourself in a more positive light.

Drop your baggage.

It is very possible that resentment and bitterness from your past are standing in the way of being truly happy. Every one of us has been through a difficult childhood, failed relationship, painful loss, unexpected tragedy, or some other hurtful experience that has left us feeling sad or resentful — perhaps for many years. However, to enjoy life to its fullest extent, it is time to commit to leaving that baggage behind.

The fact is, we cannot change the past. We can decide, however, not to let painful memories and unresolved anger affect our current happiness or relationships.

Emotional baggage can be imagined just like physical luggage — it is weighing you down, so feel free to set it down and move on. When you let go of bitterness about past events, you are free to embrace new opportunities, rebuild trust, enjoy the company of others, and give wholly of yourself.

While letting go of a hurtful past is not always easy or quick, you can make the conscious decision to begin leaving baggage behind, today.

What is one thing you are angry or bitter about? Write a letter to the person or situation that details all the reasons for your resentment. Consider this the first step to letting go of this baggage.

How did it feel to write this letter? Do you feel more free from your baggage? What is the next step you will take to help you let go?

Write a poem.

You don't have to be a professional writer to benefit from writing poetry. While people often believe that poetry is difficult, it is actually one of the most liberating, cathartic forms of art you can do.

Writing poetry can reveal your innermost feelings and fears, provide clarity, and offer comfort. Opening yourself up with words and metaphors can be inspirational and even therapeutic. In the U.S., there is actually a National Association for Poetry Therapy, and *The Journal of the American Medical Association* has published a section called "Poetry in Medicine," featuring poems by cancer patients and doctors. Many of these people explained that creating poetry helped them delve into their hopes and fears, as well as feel less isolated.

So, to explore your deepest feelings (as well as your creative side), write a poem. It can be any type or style you like, and it doesn't have to rhyme or even be very long. You will find poetry a wonderful means of expression that leads to clarity and discovery.

What are your experiences with writing poetry, either in your free time, in school, or otherwise? How did you enjoy it?

Write a poem on any topic that inspires you right now.

How did it feel to create that poem?

Find a community within your community.

Part of enjoying life is belonging to a community or social group filled with people you relate to.

Find a small community within your larger one, such as a yoga class, sports team, book club, or group that is learning to speak French. Any group, team, club, or organization that you identify with can enrich your life by introducing you to new people.

MeetUp.com is a wonderful online resource for finding community groups in your area — anything from software engineers to hiking enthusiasts to bulldog owners. The site allows you to sign up for as many groups as interest you and attend "meet ups" where you can network and enjoy the company of people with your same interests and lifestyle.

Feeling like a part of something bigger than you and socializing with people you relate to will bring you much happiness.

Do you currently belong to any community groups or social clubs?

_____

_____

_____

_____

_____

Do some research and record a list of group, clubs, teams, or organizations you could benefit from joining. Commit yourself to trying at least one of these new groups.

_____

_____

_____

_____

_____

_____

_____

_____

Describe your experience. How did it feel to meet people who reflected your similar interests? Did you feel a sense of inclusion?

_____

_____

_____

_____

_____

_____

Rekindle a long-lost friendship.

Many people have lost touch with friends who were once near and dear. School, marriage, and relocation may have sent you in different directions, although you still care deeply for one another. Even if you have not talked to the person in many years, it can be very rewarding to reach out and rekindle the friendship.

The Internet makes it easier than ever to regain contact with a long-lost friend. With a bit of searching, you should be able to find an email, phone number, or address for the person.

No matter what life circumstances drove you apart, you should apologize for the time lost. Explain that you have missed the person and would like to reestablish the friendship. Share a bit about what is going on in your life to spark conversation.

True friendship should endure through distance, time, and circumstance. If you do successfully reconnect with an old friend, appreciate the opportunity for a second chance by making the most of it!

What friend from your past would you like to reconnect with? How did you lose touch?

Decide what you want to say when you contact your long-lost friend. Write down why you hope to rekindle the friendship, as well as what you hope to gain from reconnecting.

Reflect on the experience of attempting to rekindle this friendship. Did it go as planned? Were you pleased or disappointed?

Curl up with a good read.

Taking some time with a good book or magazine provides many benefits to your health and happiness — reading reduces anxiety, helps you unwind, and gives you an escape from reality. Additionally, reading stimulates the brain and benefits memory.

Better still, curling up with a good book indicates that you are setting some time aside just for you. You should never feel guilty about "neglecting" other duties to make time for yourself — especially a pastime with so many health habits.

Have friends or coworkers who have similar tastes recommend good books or magazines you can pick up. You can even stock up on reading material by purchasing used books in great condition online.

So take the time to read — you'll be pleasantly surprised at how it relaxes you and improves your mood in just a few minutes.

How often do you read? Do you read every day? Every week? Or do you feel you don't have enough time to read?

Make a list of the books and/or magazines you would like to get. Cross them off your list as you read them.

Have you successfully found time to read? How has reading helped you unwind or de-stress?

SECRET 94

Tackle something you've been putting off.

Everyone has projects or tasks they have been putting off until some unknown date in the future. Perhaps it is a small task, like taking a pair of pants to the tailor; or perhaps it is a larger, more daunting effort, such as cleaning your garage.

No matter the size or scope of the project, make it a point to tackle one thing you have been putting off, because procrastination can lead to feeling overwhelmed and unaccomplished. As American psychologist and philosopher William James once said, "Nothing is so fatiguing as the eternal hanging on of an uncompleted task." Truly, unfinished business can weigh on your mind.

Don't let procrastination drag you down. Set a deadline for completing or following through with one task that has been looming and stick to that deadline as if it were an appointment you can't cancel. You will feel so relieved and relaxed when you tackle the task, cross it off your list, and put it out of your mind.

How badly do you procrastinate?

_____

_____

_____

_____

_____

Write down 3 things you have been meaning to do but have put off. Next, detail how you will tackle these tasks.

1. _____

_____

_____

2. _____

_____

_____

3. _____

_____

_____

How did completing the task or tasks make you feel?

_____

_____

_____

_____

_____

Learn the art of compromise.

Happy people with successful careers, friendships, and relationships are highly skilled in the art of compromise. Compromise requires patience, commitment, maturity, and empathy. Compromising is not a sign of weakness, but one of strength. You have to be willing to let go of the scorecard and consider the greater good. You must be willing to modify your stance or recognize when an issue is so important to you that you can't change your opinion, but are open to considering another viewpoint. Finally, in compromise, you must be open to giving more than you receive.

Your ability to see where your friend, boss, or spouse is coming from lets you make statements such as, "You have an interesting point of view," "I understand why you feel that way," or "Let's find a solution we're both comfortable with." Understanding the art of compromise helps you respond to another person's opposing point of view in a kind, sincere, and respectful way.

Compromise involves a give-and-take negotiation in which each party receives something satisfying. Mastering this art is crucial to happiness in your job, friendships, and romantic life, so start compromising today.

Are you skilled at compromise? Or is compromise with friends, family, and coworkers something you find difficult? Is there a particular person you have trouble compromising with?

Think of a scenario in your life where you would need to come to a compromise. Then, describe what you might do or say to find a solution that works for both parties.

Reflect on the most recent time when you had to compromise. How did it go, and what was the end result?

Choose a fitness event and work toward it.

It can be difficult to stay motivated to exercise at times. However, choosing a fitness event that is a few months away and working toward it is a great way to stay active and accomplish something that makes you feel great.

Start small, such as with a 5k run/walk or 20k bicycle ride. Once you get comfortable and feel the rush of completing an event, you can work your way to bigger events like a half-marathon or mini-triathlon.

Many charities raise donations with fitness events, for instance the Avon Walk for Breast Cancer and the Dr. Seuss Walk for Literacy. Participating in these events will not only give you a goal to work toward that will improve your fitness; it will also raise funds for a worthy cause.

Check your local gym or sports supply store for a list of events in your area. Or, visit www.active.com, which lets you search and register online for races, team sports, and recreational activities in your area. Additionally, you can find groups to train with for the event — a great way to meet new people who share your fitness goals!

Have you ever participated in or trained for a fitness event in the past? Describe it and how you felt afterward.

Spend some time researching events in your area that are a few months away. Make a list of those that appeal to you and the dates they are happening.

Reflect on working toward your fitness event. Was it easy to stay motivated as the date neared? Did you meet new people during training? How did it feel to complete the event?

Redefine yourself!

How do you define yourself? Consider this question carefully. Do you define yourself with qualities that can change or falter, such as being "pretty" or "a genius." Or, do you define yourself through things largely outside of your control, such as a relationship or job? Unfortunately, building your self-image on those things makes for very unstable ground. You must learn to redefine yourself as more than a few bullet points in order to stay happy and fulfilled throughout your life.

Take, for example, Julie Wainwright, the former CEO of Pets.com, which came to represent the crash and burn of the Dotcom era in the '90s. When she closed her company in 2000, her name became synonymous with failure. Whereas she had always defined herself as the "smart girl" who could solve any problem, she was suddenly faced with a sinking ship she couldn't save. As fate would have it, her husband filed for a divorce that same week. Her definition of herself as a "married woman," also ended. However, over time, Wainwright learned to redefine herself in new terms — loving, creative and artistic, and able to triumph over adversity.

Redefining yourself in terms of unique, real qualities helps you build a solid foundation for who you are. With this definition, you will be strong enough to weather any storm.

Finish this sentence: "I define myself as ..."

Do you recognize terms, words, or phrases you use to define yourself that are unstable or give a false sense of security? Can you dig deeper to replace or rework them?

How do you anticipate your definition of yourself will change over time?

Learn from past missteps.

You have probably heard successful people talk about how the mistakes in their lives turned into opportunities for growth. This should be true in your personal life, business situations, and all relationships. You will falter. The goal is to learn from past missteps and use them as learning experiences and opportunities to benefit.

If a romantic relationship ends, or you lose your job, you may be tempted to wallow in disappointment. However, these are actually chances to learn why things did not work out as you planned and to improve yourself for the next venture.

Mistakes teach us to live unselfishly, be curious, accept responsibility, and grow. People who view life as a learning and growing process will bounce back from every misstep even stronger and with a greater appreciation for life.

Describe the last time you made a major mistake in your life.

Now, think about that misstep as a learning and growing experience — mistakes often close one door to open another. What positive lessons do you take away from the situation?

Can you reflect on the ways you have actually benefited from your mistake?

Rest assured,
there is a plan for you.

Whether you believe in God, the universe, or the power of destiny, rest assured that there is a plan for you and your life. You do not need to have the answers every step of the way. As this book teaches you, cultivating relationships with others and yourself, reaching out to people in need, planning ahead, and even making mistakes are all important aspects of life.

Diving into life and maintaining a positive perspective help you make the most of each day, but, in the end, there is a plan for you. Life guides you in different directions and offers you choices and opportunities, and it is up to you to take them and make the most of them.

Do not worry that you don't know where you will be in 10 years, or that you haven't found your soulmate or dream job. Simply look forward with an open heart and mind, allowing you to best navigate the path that is laid out for you.

How often do you worry about the direction or purpose of your life? Is this a stressful thing for you?

Describe a time when you felt life's plan in action.

How do you feel when you think about the fact that there is a plan for you?

Enjoy life and be happy!

Many times, happiness is simply a matter of making a few changes to your attitude, perspective, and lifestyle.

While we are often conditioned to feel negative, bitter, and competitive in our daily lives, there is much beauty and joy to be appreciated in everything we experience and everyone we come across. You will find that even difficult situations and hardship are tests of strength, character, and a positive attitude.

There are times when simply being active or trying something new can help you enjoy life to the fullest. There are times when nurturing the relationships you have with others will give you courage, peace, and happiness. And, still, there are times when being quiet with your thoughts and enjoying alone time will make you the happiest. Life is not necessarily what is given to us, but what we make of it and do with it.

As writer Leo Tolstoy once said, "If you want to be happy: be." Appreciate the opportunities for joy around you, and you will have taken a major step toward loving life every day.

What do you believe was your number one obstacle to happiness and enjoying life prior to picking up this book?

What are the most important secrets this book has given you for loving life and being happy?

Describe how you feel after learning the secrets in this book. Comforted, empowered, relieved, excited?

CONCLUSION

After reading this book you should feel excited about your prospects for happiness. As this book shows, loving life is not about what you have or don't have, but about your attitude and approach to the daily joys that surround all of us.

As the secrets and exercises in this book demonstrate, happiness is always within reach. We all know that sadness and setbacks are a part of life. But they don't need to keep you down. Focus on the opportunities that lie ahead of you.

Practicing the principles in this book and completing the exercises will make a real difference in how you feel. It is not enough to read this book one time and forget what you have read. You should refer back regularly to the secrets, as well as your journal responses, to remind you of how to love life. And, you may be pleasantly surprised when you reread old journal entries and see how much progress you are making!

Open yourself up to the positive and proactive ways of living that are found in this book. As Henry David Thoreau once wrote, "You must live in the present, launch yourself on every wave, find your eternity in each moment. Fools stand on their island of opportunities and look toward another land. There is no other land; there is no other life but this." So start practicing these secrets today! Soon enough, the new ways to view and live life outlined in this book will become second nature to you. You will find yourself experiencing and loving your life more than you ever thought possible!